Giving Birth To God

To John –
    May you grow ever
deeper into the love that
is God And may you be

a blessing to many.

                Mother Clare

Mother Mary

Giving Birth To God

✦

A Woman's Path To Enlightenment

Mother Clare Watts

iUniverse, Inc.

New York Lincoln Shanghai

Giving Birth To God
A Woman's Path To Enlightenment

iUniverse, Inc.

For information address:
iUniverse, Inc.
2021 Pine Lake Road, Suite 100
Lincoln, NE 68512
www.iuniverse.com

ISBN: 0-595-28337-3 (pbk)
ISBN: 0-595-74837-6 (cloth)

Printed in the United States of America

I dedicate this book to Mother Mary, my teacher, guide, and beloved spiritual Mother, who has with immeasurable patience and love led me through all the experiences that fill these pages. It was under her guidance and direction that this book came about. She was the first woman to fully take on spiritual mastery, and surpasses all others in the depth of that mastery and love. It is my great hope that through this book many may open to and come to know her love and her healing power. I give my eternal love and appreciation to her and to my Master Jesus.

Contents

INTRODUCTION

I offer this, my spiritual life story, with the hope that it will be a blessing and an aid to others. My voyage took me from missionary parents through yogic ashrams and a Sufi school, through ups and downs in mystical Christian training, through deep and holy initiations and powerful mystical ordinations into the priesthood, and later, into spiritual mastery. I now serve as a founder and a director of the Order of Christ/Sophia. My work is to give to others what was so freely given to me. I therefore offer this story of my path to God for all those who are seeking or longing for the spiritual path, or simply wondering what it is all about. I give it as a beacon in the night, to point a direction and to give hope to the travelers along the path. As is written on the mausoleum of the great Sufi poet Rumi:

> Come, come, whoever you are,
> Wanderer, worshipper, lover of leaving, it doesn't matter.
> Ours is not a caravan of despair.
> Come, come, even if you have broken your vow a thousand times,
> Come, come yet again, come!

1

THE FIRST SIGNS OF THE CALLING: REFLECTION ON THE EARLY LIFE

What is firmly established cannot be uprooted
What is firmly grasped cannot slip away
It will be honored from generation to generation.

—Lao Tsu, *Tao Te Ching*

I walked out of Master Peter's house in Bloomington, Indiana, into a brisk winter morning. It was December 22, 1982. The previous evening's mystical Christian initiation seemed to be affecting my vision. The colors of the trees and bushes, the sparkle of the rain on the asphalt, the hues of blue and pink in the morning sky, all appeared brighter and as if boasting of the richness of their contrasting glories. I was still having trouble walking because I felt unsure of where my body ended, and therefore when my feet would reach the ground. I felt awkward, and a little giddy, not knowing what to make of these new sensations in my body. The stillness in my mind was quite foreign given my usual state of active cogitating. Fortunately, my friend Nancy was going to be driving me home. As I climbed into the car, the texture of the seat upholstery caught my attention. It seemed softer than before as I noticed that my hands were exquisitely sensitive to the feeling of each different surface that they encountered. My head felt as if its dimensions and even its consistency were altered. Master Peter told Nancy before she and I left that I was in a highly altered state and to simply let me be silent and inward on our long drive home.

Riding in the car, I saw as well as felt light pouring out of my body. It emanated from my hands, creating a white glow around them. I felt the light streaming from my head and face, while it continued to energize my body and still my mind. I found it hard to tell where my body's boundaries were, because the light was the same both inside and around my body. The light seemed to be working in every cell of my physical being. It stimulated in me a sense of exhilaration, not as emotions are exhilarating, but rather as if I was being irradiated with energy of a much higher vibration and consciousness than I had ever known before. I felt it simultaneously penetrate and change the cells of my mind and heart, causing me to think and feel in a whole new way. I felt an equanimity, a serene sense of balance and stillness in my heart and mind, as if I had entered another world. In this new world, stillness, peace, and beautiful white light were the building blocks of all that existed, and joined together they now permeated my body, my thoughts, and my feelings. "So this is the experience of illumination!" I thought to myself. During the drive home to central Kentucky, where my family and I lived, I drank in the beauty of nature along the highway. Colors looked brighter, contrasts clearer, and the perfect harmony between plants and trees, sky and hills, brooks and rivers, flooded my senses and filled me with awe. I pondered the wondrousness of what I received the previous evening.

When Nancy and I had arrived at Master Peter's house the night before, I thought I was simply attending a class in Christian mysticism, as I had several times previously, to be followed by a special winter solstice service. I was feeling embarrassed toward Master Peter for the previous night's phone call, in which I had confessed that I had just had an argument with my husband, Sal, in which I had felt so much anger and hurt that I wanted to physically attack and harm him. Master Peter had laughed and talked me down from my anger. After that phone call, I certainly was not expecting my teacher to give me the immense gift of the initiation of illumination. And yet he did. Later I came to understand that it is not unusual for people to feel overwhelmed with anger and hurt as they draw close to readiness for an initiation. This is the meaning behind the metaphor "the darkest hour is just before dawn." The initiation of illumination was the dawning of the spiritual light within my being, and the immense anger I felt toward my husband was that dark hour immediately preceding it. In the following years, I learned about this and many other spiritual phenomena, but now I only felt humbled and grateful that God did not reject me, and my spiritual teacher still accepted me though in my own view I felt so flawed.

At the end of the solstice service, Master Peter brought me up to the altar and called down the light of Christ into my being until it completely filled my body, my heart, and my mind. Master Peter had mentioned the initiation of illumination a few times and had somewhat explained how he and the other teachers in this mystical Christian order initiated students when they became ready. He said that there is a strict taboo against saying too much about any of the initiations, to prevent the initiate from having concepts and expectations that can interfere with their ability to be open and simply receive what is given. The experience was unimaginable and quite indescribable. The spiritual light transported me into another state of being that was peaceful and clear, and in which I felt so very loved by God, by Jesus, and by Mary. I felt safer than I had ever felt before and filled with a certainty that I would always be provided for as long as I stayed in and near this light of Christ. I spent the night in the chapel, overwhelmed with the reality of the light that now had taken up residence inside of me. I felt with immense clarity that this light was a gift of God's grace, rather than something I could have ever earned. Though I had been meditating for years, this new state of being filled with light clearly was immensely greater than anything I had ever experienced. Gratitude flooded my heart and I sat back in my seat contemplating the glory of God and how little I had known about who God is and what God does.

Nancy drove in silence. I appreciated the support she lent me by allowing me to stay inside of my experience. My mind wandered back over my entire life. I was now 29 years old. I reviewed how I had come to this time and place. Here, in a house that looked liked any other, in a regular neighborhood of Bloomington, Indiana, this Christian master teacher, Master Peter, a man who many knew only as a family man and a psychologist, had donned his white teacher robes and had called down forces from on high. Via the filling of my being with light, I knew he had changed my life. I now knew with a certainty that I could never have imagined that I was made of light, that spiritual power moves and changes us, even our bodies, and that we can have a direct relationship with the beings that come to us from the spiritual world. What forces and events in my life had led up to my receiving this great spiritual gift at this particular time? Had I been searching and preparing for this all my life? Were there clues in my earlier life that I was to enter upon a mystical path to God? Master Peter had told me that the experience was called an initiation because it was the beginning of the next leg of my journey toward God. If this was just a beginning, then where was I headed? Though I tried to imagine what might come my way on this mystical spiritual journey, I felt an inner directive suggesting I steer clear of any such speculation. I could, however, review the road I had already traveled. As the sun rose higher in the sky and the car engine hummed steadily, basking in the brilliance of the light that filled my body and mind, I closed my eyes and began a retrospection of my life.

Early Life in Switzerland

I was born in 1954 in Zurich, Switzerland. My parents were Americans, sent to Switzerland to start a theological seminary. Growing up on a seminary campus staffed by missionaries induced mixed feelings in my youthful heart. Missionaries are driven by a need to make the world a better place. I also felt such a calling from a very young age. Yet I never thought that my path would be like theirs. I learned from my parents to bless and thank God for my food and to be grateful for all that is given to me; I learned to give 10 percent of whatever I received back to God as a tithe; and I saw that I needed to strive to determine what God's plan was for me, and I should follow it wherever it might take me. These were wonderful teachings for which I am always grateful. However, I felt conflicted about some of the other expressions of missionary Christianity that I saw around me. I mistrusted those who were too sweet. I could also not believe that God wanted us to always be somber. My parents inspired me through the depth of their commitment and their joy in serving God. Some of the other missionaries exemplified what I never wanted to be. They seemed false and unhappy, trying too hard to be "good" and "nice." As I grew up, I moved away from many of the teachings of the denomination in which I was raised, but the positive lessons I had learned stayed as a bedrock beneath my feet, a solid structure upon which I was to build my spiritual life.

One of my earliest attempts at making the world a better place began with my deep love for chocolate. Living in Switzerland, the country best known for making wonderful chocolates, may well have contributed to my feeling that chocolate was important. It was my impression that all candy was made for children, as it was always offered to us as a reward and when visiting others. I remember thinking that adults only ate it occasionally, when it was around. Each day, walking to kindergarten, I passed by a grocery store, the only one in the small town where I lived. Every time I passed by it, I thought about all the chocolate in the store, and how much my friends and I longed for it. As I pondered this with all the capacity my five-year old mind could muster, it seemed wrong to me that chocolate cost money. Everyone knows children do not have money.

One day I decided that it was up to me to rectify this situation. I asked my little friends who walked home from kindergarten with me what they wanted from the store. Each of them told me, and I went into the store and came out with something tasty for everyone hidden under my coat. We all enjoyed it so much that I repeated my not-so-selfless Robin Hood routine for the "poor" children each day, until some days later I was caught. When I was apprehended, I still acted quite self-righteous, though I also felt guilty about lying to my mother when she had queried me about the source of the daily evidence of chocolate on my face. And yet I believed somewhere in my heart that the situation of children not having access to chocolate was wrong, and *someone* had to do something about it. After all, I was only five, and my understanding of a holy cause that was worth fighting for was still quite limited.

Later the same year, I made another effort to rid the world of evil. Construction workers had dug a ditch the entire length of the block on which we lived. The workers left full liter-bottles of beer throughout the ditch overnight to keep them cool and ready for the next day. My parents' denomination did not approve of drinking alcohol, and I, in my young heart, believed I was seeing evidence of Satan's work displayed right before my eyes. In a brave moment, I went up and down the block and broke every bottle in the ditch. I was proud to be such a soldier for God. I went in the house and braggingly told my mother what I had done. She and my father were appalled, especially since they had to replace all the workers' beer the next day. But they did see that I truly believed I had been ridding the world of evil, and I was not punished for it. I could not understand, however, why they did not support my action.

When I was seven years old, during our furlough in North Carolina, I attended a large revival service at a missionary conference. I wanted to make public my desire to give my life to Jesus, and I knew, now that I was seven, that I could do so. When the preacher asked if anyone wanted to come forward and accept Jesus as their savior, and as the congregation beautifully sang "Just as I am Without a Plea," I squeezed past all the people in our pew. I walked down the long aisle to the front, where I told the minister that I wanted to give my life to Jesus. The minister prayed with me and accepted me into the fold. I was so happy to finally have been able to take that step, and I felt so much love for Jesus that I thought I would burst. Unbeknownst to me, this was to constitute the first step on the winding path that would, in time, lead me onto the way of the mystics, and into the initiation of illumination.

Children, Souls, and Reincarnation

What is it in children's hearts and souls that makes them so open to God, and if they are introduced to Jesus and Mary, to them, too? You might think that children are simply too young to distinguish reality from fantasy and can get excited about all kinds of unseen things, like fairies, angels, and even ghosts and goblins. "They have great imaginations," is what adults usually say about the things children see and experience that adults don't. Or might children still be more in touch with their souls, and therefore need very little stimulation to let the purposes and desires of their souls into their hearts and minds? Could the ancients possibly have been right when they said that each human being has a soul, and within that soul, a core that is pure God? In order to have a sense of what I mean when I suggest that children may be more in touch with their souls, we will need to examine what is a soul, and from where does it come.

The great masters of old, of all traditions, have told us that our souls are, in fact, eternal. Just as physics teaches us that matter cannot be created or destroyed, but can only be changed, so it is with our souls. Only God can create matter, and only God can create a soul. The belief in reincarnation is still not widely held or understood in the Western world. I do not expect you to simply take my word that our souls return many times to earth as truth. But I do ask you, for now, to at least consider it a possibility. Reincarnation is not the caricature people have made of it by saying that you may come back as your Aunt Sallie's arthritic Chihuahua or that you must have been some great personage of times past. It is a complex matter that I trust you will understand better through stories from my and my children's lives. You may well find that when you understand reincarnation, your life makes much more sense and the situations people are born into and experiences they encounter feel much fairer and full of wisdom than before. As you read my stories, you will see how I came to feel that I know reincarnation is true.

According to the teachings of reincarnation, we have all had many lives; our souls have been formed and affected by the many experiences we have had on earth. Though in the West we often think of the belief in reincarnation as belonging only to the Eastern religions, it has actually been an integral part of the teachings of both East and West. Two references still stand in the New Testament today that to some readers, at least, point to Jesus' acceptance of the teaching of reincarnation. In Matthew 17:11-13 Jesus' disciples ask him about the prophecy regarding the coming of the Messiah. The prophecy stated that Elijah was to *return* before the Messiah came, in order to prepare the way for the Messiah. "Jesus said: 'But I tell you that Elijah *has already come*, and they did not recognize him, but they did to him whatever they pleased.' *Then the disciples understood that Jesus was speaking to them about John the Baptist.*" So Jesus was saying that Elijah came back as John the Baptist.

In the New Testament, in John 9:1-3, the issue comes up again. "As Jesus walked along, he saw a man blind from birth. The disciples asked him, 'Rabbi, who sinned, this man or his parents, that he was born blind?' Jesus answered, 'Neither this man nor his parents sinned; he was born blind so that God's works might be revealed in him.'" Note that Jesus did not say that reincarnation was a false teaching. He said that in this case the blindness was not due to anyone's sin, but for another purpose. If he considered reincarnation an untruth, why did he not say so? Though these are the only two instances we have now in the New Testament that point to Jesus' agreeing with reincarnation as a teaching, it is quite possible that there were other references to reincarnation that the Church edited out. Many things were changed in the books that currently make up the New Testament, so the above references may have been altered as well. The only way anyone could know for sure is if he or she could either get an answer on the matter from God directly, or if he or she could see into his or her own past, before birth. I encourage those of you who want to learn how to access your own pre-birth past to seek answers through one or both of those means. Only then will you be able to rest assured that what you believe is true.

If, indeed, our souls are eternal and we have incarnated many times before, then it would stand to reason that children could be closer to the memory of themselves as eternal beings. Especially before they begin to be educated into reasoning and logic, they can feel the truth emanating from inside. Before they are taught to ignore all but what the material eyes can see or the mind can reason out, many children have more of an open door to the world that adults call "the unseen." If their soul has a calling to service imprinted upon it, a child can feel that very early in life. If she does not allow the world to crust over it, she will still hear that calling once she is grown.

Speaking in Tongues, a Visit With the Devil, and a Religious Affinity From Another Life

When I was nine, my father exchanged jobs for nine months with a professor at a seminary in Beirut, Lebanon. While living there, I told the pastor from the church we attended that I wanted to be baptized. In my family's denomination, baptism was not given to infants, but rather to those old enough to understand such a commitment to God. Our pastor considered me to be old enough. The baptism was in the form of total immersion in a pool made especially for that purpose in the church. I felt intuitively that this was another step along my way to God. Yet even at this early age, I noticed that the spiritual life I found in this denomination seemed enough for my parents and other church members, yet already felt somehow lacking to me. A fire burned inside my heart that was distressing, because it told me that this kind of religious practice would never be enough. I knew of nothing else, so what did it all mean? Was I doing something wrong to not be satisfied with the spiritual opportunities that my church offered? I did love the hymns, and I often choked up when we sang of Jesus' love and of His dying for us. I was only nine, and it was easy to believe in and love Jesus. For now, that was all I could do. When I was 13, we were once again on furlough in the US. I went to stay with my cousin and her parents in Austin, Texas. I did not know before I went that my aunt and uncle were leaders of a charismatic community there. Charismatics are Christians from any denomination who seek to work with the Holy Spirit and to be open to receive the sacred gifts that are spoken of in the New Testament. My aunt and uncle hosted charismatic prayer meetings in their house. My cousin invited me to come with her to such a meeting shortly after I arrived. They gave me no information about what to expect but simply invited me to come and see.

Before I knew what was happening to me, I found myself speaking in tongues. In his writings, St. Paul called this practice one of the gifts of the Spirit. As it is applied today in charismatic groups, speaking in tongues involves people feeling the Spirit of God come over them and allowing what sounds like nonsense words to come from their mouths as they are caught up in prayer. This "speaking in the Spirit" can be very exhilarating for the person doing it, and sometimes someone else present can "interpret," meaning they are given another gift by the Holy Spirit, the "interpretation of tongues." With interpretation, that which is said in tongues sometimes turns out to be a divine message for someone else in the room, a prophesy of things to come, or just a prayer of praise and glory to God. Some messages offered reassurance to a particular person about a situation about which they had prayed. Some were warnings that a person needed to follow if he or she were to stay safe and in accord with God's will for them. Some were words of blessing and guidance for a person's life.

I was amazed to find myself actually caught up in the experience. It seemed to take me over, and I was full of awe and gratitude to have discovered such a wonderful way to pray. In this group, people often asked for healing prayers. Other attendees laid their hands on the one asking for the blessing, with some people praying in tongues and others praying in English. I witnessed numerous healings during my six-week stay with my cousin, and became quite immersed in this life in the Spirit. There were virtually daily opportunities to give healing prayers to someone in need. I began to feel quite at home in this active prayer and healing life. I loved how alive it was, and how miracles seemed to be occurring every day when people came together to pray in this dynamic way. I felt healing powers flow through me as I laid my hands on each person in need.

One night my cousin and I were kneeling on opposite sides of our double bed, saying our evening prayers, when both of us had the same vision of a huge figure we knew to be the devil looming over us. As each of us struggled to elude his powers, we must have made strange noises, because my aunt and uncle came in and hauled us out of the room. The energy in the room was so bad that my relatives called in a Catholic priest to drive out the darkness that still seemed to linger there.

Though the devil experience was somewhat frightening, it did not stop my deep involvement with the group. It taught me that if I was to actively engage with the spiritual world, I would need to know how to protect myself from any forms of darkness I might encounter there. Later in life, I was happy to learn how to surround myself with divine light whenever I perceived a negative energy to be present. For the meantime, I was told to never indulge such dark energies but rather to ask Jesus to take them away immediately. I loved being with these people and praying with them because it was exciting, never dull. This seemed more like what I had hoped for in my spiritual life. But before long it was time for my family to return to Switzerland. Once there, I could not find a charismatic group to join. After trying to continue in the practice on my own, I fell away from it a few months after returning from the USA. I found that I did not have enough experience to continue the practice without the support and company of the group. I felt deep sadness to no longer have this in my life. However, the experience did leave me knowing that there were more intensive ways to relate to God than what I found in the Protestant church we attended. For a while, I occasionally continued to pray in tongues during my own prayer time. I was also beginning to date, and though my conscience tried to keep my prayer life most important, somehow usually boys won out on my list of priorities.

Around this same time, I had my first experience of a Catholic mass. My best friend had invited me to go with her to her church. My initial reaction to seeing the candles, smelling the incense, and hearing the chanting was, "*This* is what church is supposed to look, smell, and sound like." I didn't know how to explain myself, but the feeling came from deep inside. I seemed to be recognizing something I had long forgotten. I felt at home there. Years later, when I understood reincarnation and began to get a sense of my past lives, I understood that I had those feelings in my first visit to a Catholic Church because I had spent several lifetimes living in Catholic monasteries. The smells and sights tapped into memories that lay imprinted on my soul and aroused a deep sense of recognition and attraction to the Catholic mass and way of life.

These early experiences with God were to hold me over as I dove into my tumultuous teen years. The innocence of childhood beliefs were supplanted by a powerful rebellion against all that my parents stood for and did. These were the bridge years through which all must pass, and through which I charged with gusto, learning, growing and, of course, getting deeply hurt. If God was to be a part of my life in the future, I felt sure it would not be through a church. My defiance of the outer forms of Christianity was only a veil over my inner knowing that God was real, and that I wanted to find God and come to know God in some way that felt right to me. What form that would take, I could not even imagine. I did know that I did not want to be a part of a stodgy, pious-looking group of people who were all trying to be good. I did not want to be good. I was a teenager, and the 1960s revolution was in full swing. I did not want to miss a beat. I assumed I could sort out "the God thing" later. For now, there was a revolution to support, and I intended on participating in it fully.

2

THE SOUL'S DEEPEST DESIRE: TO SEE AND KNOW GOD

Siddhartha Introduces the Concept of a Spiritual Path

God's servants will worship God; they will see God's face, and God's name will be on their foreheads.

—New Testament, *Revelations 22:3-4*

Through age 13 I attended Swiss schools where the instruction was quite rigid and disciplined. This style of education did not suit my freewheeling, rebellious teenage spirit. When I was 14, I enrolled in an American high school near Zurich. Classes often had as few as eight students, and free thought was, for the most part, greatly encouraged. This felt much better to me, even though I had never written a creative paper before, as the Swiss did not give such assignments. Nor had I ever written anything in English (other than letters to my grandparents).

My first English class assignment was to read the initial two chapters of Genesis as literature and write a paper on them. I was amazed, excited, and delighted to enter into discussions and investigations of how to understand creation, the Bible, God, and life in very different ways. This was not a theology class. The teacher was not interested in Genesis as a religious text. Instead, he sought to stimulate our thinking and make us question our assumptions. The next paper he assigned was on the book of Job, also from the Old Testament. I was enthralled by Job's conclusion at the end of the story, and I wrote a passionate paper on it. Because the teacher recognized how deeply engrossed I was with these matters of life and death, God and humans, he handed me the book *Siddhartha*, by Herman

Hesse and suggested I read it. That book became the foundation upon which I was to build my spiritual search and consequent life.

Siddhartha is Hesse's rendition of the life of Gautama Buddha. My heart leapt with joy and recognition as I read about the young Siddhartha's quest and his development and training along the spiritual path. "I knew it!" I exclaimed. "I knew there had to be more than what I have been exposed to so far!" I was thrilled to hear about the existence of an actual spiritual path that had very specific levels of training and development, and that one could strive to grow to the heights of heaven and into the presence of God. A number of years passed before I came to understand the true nature of the relationship between God and soul, what the soul is, and what souls come to earth to do.

What is a Soul and What is its Relationship With God?

We are placed in bodies and on earth in order to have the opportunity, through knowing God, to become like God. We are, therefore, souls that have bodies, rather than, as we commonly think, bodies that have souls. Theologians and philosophers have written and conjectured reams and reams about the human soul. With the advent of Carl Jung and Jungian psychology, which for the first time addressed issues of the soul in psychological terms, even more confusion seems to have come into the subject. The word "soul" is now used so broadly that it is in danger of losing all meaning. Despite this confusion, the soul is real and can be perceived. Over the years of my training, I have come to have a direct experience of my soul, and the souls of others. I *know* what and where the soul is and what it looks like because I can see it. I am not unique in this ability. People who have developed enough spiritual sight, and have had a master teacher bring them into Self-realization, will be able to see their own souls and their God-Selves. They may also be able to come to see other people's souls and God-Selves over time.

The soul and the God-Self constitute that which is eternal in humans. The God-Self is at the core of the soul, and is pure God. A friend once told me the following story: Back when the world was being created, God was pondering how He/She could set it up so that, when humans were ready, they would be able to find God. God called a council of the Great Ones and asked for their input. "Where shall I hide Myself so that humans will not find me too soon, before they are ready, and yet will be able to find Me when they have been properly prepared?" All the Great Ones thought deep thoughts, and then came up with some suggestions. "Maybe if You hide Yourself at the bottom of the sea, by the time they are able to go there, they will be ready to find You." "Maybe if You hide

Yourself at the top of the highest mountains, by the time they are able to go there, they will be ready to find You." But each idea, once examined, was determined to be inadequate as a guarantee that humans would be truly ready to find God when they could go to that geographical location. Finally God exclaimed: "I know! I will hide Myself inside human beings. It is the very last place they will look. And when they look there, they will be ready to find Me."

Because the God-Self is pure God, it is the same in every person. Why do we call it Self if it is pure God? The profound truth is that we are all nothing less than a variety of expressions of God Itself. By using the word "Self" we force ourselves to confront this great mystical and perplexing truth: We actually *are* pure God, Who wishes to express through the shell of our souls, which surround that God at our center. This great being within us has all the power of the Creator, and all the Creator's knowing, wisdom, love, and life inside of it. Think of how a cell from your body has the DNA of your entire body. That cell is a tiny microcosm of you. The relationship between the God-Self and the God of all is the same as the relationship between a cell in your body and your entire body. The God-Self is a tiny microcosm of the great God. This part of us that is pure God is not located in the human brain, as many might guess, but rather in the proximity of the solar plexus. When spiritual seekers are brought into the Presence of that God at their center through the aid of a master teacher, who can see when a student is ready, they are then able to access the wisdom and guidance of that great being much more clearly. They can also begin to know God through the direct contact that then becomes available to them.

If the Self is pure God, what is the soul? The soul envelops the Self like a sheath. Unlike the Self, which is the same in each person, the soul is different in each of us. It has been impacted and formed through the many experiences we have had since we were created, and has become unique in its expression of God. Each soul longs to see and know God, and to enter into an ecstatic embrace with what mystics say is its true lover, its divine spouse.

Each soul has been wonderfully shaped and formed through its many lifetimes on Earth. When a person has a particularly positive or negative experience, it makes an impact, effecting a change to the soul due to that experience. In subsequent lives, we carry with us some hopes, fears, and patterns of behavior from the past that influence us and help to form our current life. The light of the God-Self shines through the soul, causing the soul to emanate a particular color or hue. Each hue is slightly different, as each soul is unique. The variety of hues of our souls is truly a wonder to behold. However, these beautiful soul colors cannot shine through the layers of "dirt" crusting over the soul. We must, through conscious effort, peel off this dirt, which is mostly made up of our fears, resentments, and selfishness.

Can people discover all that is crusting over their souls and set about removing it themselves? Everything is possible, so this must also be possible. However, as the Sufis say, without the help of a guide a day's journey can take two hundred years. Highly trained spiritual teachers can see what is crusting over a person's soul. They can either directly or indirectly bring the student's attention to those things that need to be peeled away or transformed. This is why people's souls jump with joy when they find teachers and begin to work with them. The souls know that they are nearing a time when they, and God at their centers, will be able to shine through and fully express in those bodies, hearts, and minds.

The Capacity of Souls to be Virtuous and Their Tendency, at Times, to be Mean

All human souls were created with the same potentials and abilities, equally pure, and also with the freedom to make choices. Many people have wondered why God gave humans the ability to do evil, to be cruel, to reject God, and to refuse to love at all. In fact, God gave us absolute freedom of choice and will. From the beginning of our souls' existence, we have been making choices that over many lifetimes have brought our souls to the states they are in now. Why did God not make us so we would all be nice and good? Why didn't God create a world without the possibility of evil, where everyone loves each other and loves God?

Many people hold anger and resentment against God for allowing bad things to happen. Some blame God for all the wars humans have waged against each other, all the murder, rape, and violence that has ever been committed. They also hold God responsible for adults hurting children or not giving them enough love, for men and women hurting each other, for hatred and selfishness, jealousy and greed, addiction and depression, anxiety and loneliness. Thousands of people who are angry and suffering blame God every day for all these things. And yet, have those who blame God for giving humans the ability to do wrong thought through what it would mean if God had done otherwise? Because if they did, they would see that God had no choice if He/She wanted us to have souls and be individuals. Yes, God could have made us automatons, who could not love or grow, who could not be courageous, ingenious, creative, heroic, or gentle, and who could not seek God. These wonderful attributes can only exist if the possibility of their opposites exists as well. How can there be love, if there is not the possibility of not loving? How can there be courage, if one cannot choose it over cowardice? Every one of the virtues lives only because it is chosen over its oppos-ing evil, or lack of virtue.

We, as souls, not only need the option to be virtuous, but to not be virtuous, so that choosing virtue is meaningful. Our capacity to feel hurt, anger, and hatred actually has a positive use in our lives. Let us consider the positive uses of our capacity to have negative feelings by examining violence: Could God simply have made human souls nonviolent by nature, so that violence would never enter our minds or that we would not even have the capability of being violent? As God is omnipotent, we have to assume that God could have created humans to be inca-pable of violence. What would we have been like? Consider what is happening inside of you when you get to the point where you want to strike out and hurt someone either physically or emotionally. What prompts a person to feel that way?

Underlying most people's desire to strike out at other people is great anger. Anger arises from hurt and fear. It boils up as a defense mechanism when we sense that someone is being wronged, or is about to be wronged. It is a strong inner call to whatever action will keep the person who is perceived as being the wrongdoer from continuing to act. Without the sense of anger arising in us, we would often not notice that a wrong was taking place, and even if we noticed, we might not have the needed fiery energy to respond quickly to prevent further harm. During my early teen years, I responded in great anger and complete resis-tance to all the limitations my parents tried to put on me. My parents were, from an adult perspective, being quite reasonable in their limit setting. Only later did I come to understand why I was so immensely opposed to any signs of them possi-bly attempting to control me. In several of my past lives, my families tried to pre-vent me from entering into a spiritual life, often because it entailed leaving them and entering a monastery from which I would not be returning. I came into this life with a note to myself burned on my soul that read something like: "Do not let anyone have enough control over you to keep you from God." The anger and resistance I experienced toward my parents or school teachers when they tried to place limits on me was in fact the message I had inscribed on my soul that warned me to stay free so I could do my mission on Earth. That anger reaction, though I was unconscious of its origin at the time, was protective of my freedom. Anger can therefore be a powerfully positive force and can keep others and us safe.

What, then, can turn anger into a dangerous weapon that causes all kinds of harm? The capacity to feel anger does not cause harm. Instead, the misdirection and misuse of anger is the force behind much of the violent crime that is commit-ted. Anger is a messenger from deep within our feelings that tells us something needs resolution. If we came upon a man beating a child, and we did not feel anger, we might politely say to him, "Have you really thought about this?" Even without the rising of anger when we see an injustice, we might still pick up on a problem through intuition. But intuition often does not contain the fire that drives us to immediate action.

The feeling of righteous indignation over a great wrong moves people to take courageous actions to change those wrongs. Consider child labor, spouse and child abuse, and slavery: people finally outlawed these crimes because of that feeling of righteous indignation. That powerful indignation, which was a form of anger, arose in enough people to cause them to bring about the change. Anger gives us a signal that something must be changed. A powerful "Enough!" cries out from our gut. In fact, God gave us a great gift by endowing us with the ability to feel anger, *if* we allow that anger to move us to right the wrongs we see happening around us.

When we are hurt and do not have the opportunity, the power, or the skills to resolve the situation with the person who hurt us, we tend to get angry. When we are able to let the person who hurt us know they did so, and when that person feels sorry for hurting us, we can usually let go of our anger and heal. When people are hurt as children, they often do not have the power or skill, and therefore the opportunity, to find resolutions with the people who hurt them. They become wounded deep inside of them. As they grow up, they will likely be especially sensitive to anything that even remotely resembles the things or people who caused them that pain. Every person or situation that arouses that memory will trigger their anger. Some people become so used to withholding their anger that they themselves often do not know they have it until it is uncovered later in life, often during psychotherapy. Others let their anger fly, sometimes only onto those closest and dearest to them, sometimes onto entire segments of the population.

In similar ways, frustration, hurt, and fear are wonderful tools given to the human psyche that alert us to the fact that something needs to change. They are more reliable than the conscious mind in determining such need for change. When they arise in us, we feel our whole beings getting behind the force of change. Once again, they do not cause us to hurt other people. Instead, our inability or lack of opportunity to apply these feelings to effect change is most often the catalyst for loss of control and the eruption of violence. We need to make these feelings conscious and allow them to work together with our cognitive thinking to determine how appropriate they are and what actually needs to be done. Hurt feelings that are kept inside will inevitably cause people, in time, to turn against themselves or others.

You may then say, "Okay, so we need to have the capacity to become angry. But why were we endowed with the capacity to hate? What possible good can come from that?" You may think that hate is the opposite of love, and wonder why we can't have only the capacity to love. Hatred is actually not the opposite of love. Love and hate are similar in that they are ways to connect with other people. Fear is the opposite of love, for it allows no connection. Our capacity to hate is directly linked to our capacity to love. We are able to love someone because we are able to have different feelings about different people. If that were not so, all our relationships would be equally impersonal, equally "nice." No depth of feeling could flow between people because it isn't possible to have deep personal relationships with everyone. Would this be an acceptable definition of being "alive"? Would we really want to forfeit the possibility of enjoying deep love relationships with some people in our lives in order to keep us from the danger of hating anyone? Because we were created with the gift of being able to have profound connections of the heart with other people and God, we also had to accept the possibility of expressing that connection negatively, through hatred. Without the possibility of hatred, there would be no possibility of love.

Everything living has the potential of turning into its opposite. Carl Jung called this phenomena "enantiadromia." If we are to have the things that make life worth living and if human beings are to be exciting and full of potent heroism in small and large matters, then we must accept the possibility that some people may reverse those positive potentials and do harm with them. The first book of the Bible, Genesis, says that God made us in God's own image. God, who is all-powerful, has the potential to be a God of love or a God of wrath. God chooses to be a God of love. God hopes that we will choose to be people of love rather than of wrath. The beauty and glory is in the choosing of that which is divine and loving over that which is self-centered and lacking in divine qualities.

The Desire of the Soul to See and Know God

Each soul was created with a deep and undying desire to see and know the God within. God gave us this longing so that we would always turn back to the quest to find and know God no matter what happened to us. Many people are not yet aware that they have this longing in their souls. That is because their souls are still so crusted over with fear, resentment, and selfishness that they cannot feel that deep desire within them. But as soon as a person begins to clear the crust away, the desire will unfailingly appear. It cannot be otherwise, because that desire to know God is as central to your soul's makeup as your will to live. We were created in such a way that we cannot be truly happy without having entered into a deep and loving relationship with God. We might have everything earthly that we could want, but when we look within, we will find the underlying feeling of emptiness in that place inside of us that is reserved for our relationship with God. There is nothing—absolutely nothing else—that can fill that space.

My own awareness of wanting a relationship with God moved in and out of my consciousness as I grew up. At times it was strong, and at other times it was overshadowed by my desire to be fully engrossed in the activities of the world, and the excitement of the possibility of new experiences. The fullness of the realization that nothing else could fill that place in me that was reserved for relationship with God did not come until I was quite advanced on my spiritual path. This is the situation for many people: they grow into this knowing over the course of many years.

Why did God make us with this dire need to be whole and happy, and yet unable to be so without a solid love relationship with God? Was it selfish of God to do so? From our human vantage point, one could arrive at that conclusion. One might think that if God really loved us, He/She would have made us able to be happy by many different means, including ones that did not necessarily include a relationship with God. The human correlation would be that if we love someone truly, we might want him or her to be happy whether that person is in a relationship with us or not. That would be noble of us regarding another human being. So why doesn't the same value apply to God and the human soul? Why would God not want us to be happy without God?

If the purpose of living on earth was simply to find happiness, as many believe, then it would make sense that God, in God's love for us, would want us to be happy as easily as possible. Happiness is, in fact, *not* the reason we, as souls, were created. Considering all the trials and hazards of life on Earth, that would have been a poor plan. Only a cruel or not-too-bright God would have thought that to be a good idea. We have, instead, a whole different purpose. *We are placed in bodies and on Earth so we can come to know God. Only through knowing God will we be able to become like God.* The reason we get confused and think we are here to seek happiness is that we intuitively know that great joy is possible while being on Earth, and that we have the potential to be completely fulfilled. However, we do not know what will generate such happiness for us, and look for it in many places, such as in pizza for supper, a new clothes purchase, or a job promotion.

When we finally realize, after much pain and suffering and chasing of rainbows that nothing of Earth can make us happy, we either despair, or we begin to look to God. The earthly things we aspired to, whether a good career, a nice mate and family, and/or many material things, are all small compared to our possibilities through the development of the relationship with the God within. Each of us was created with the full potential to become masters over everything on Earth, not so that we might dominate the Earth, but so that we might bless it with consciousness. Jesus stated over and over that we were to do things as great as He did, and greater still. We were made with the capacity to truly become sons and daughters of God, in touch with our perfect divinity within. When we allow that creative power to move through us and we attune our hearts and minds to it, we are able to do whatever we put our minds and words to.

You may wonder why so few people have ever developed in that way. Did something go wrong with the plan? Actually, the plan was so long-term that we cannot even imagine it. Over many, many lifetimes, we are given the opportunity to get tired of chasing after earthly things and to dedicate ourselves to taking on the task of becoming what we were created to be: fully functioning sons and daughters of God. As such, we become filled with divine love, wisdom, and power, effecting wonderful change in the lives of the people with whom we come into contact. In just such a way, Master Peter was able to see past the apparent disarray I seemed to be in when I called him while so angry at my husband. Instead, he saw that I was in the darkness that often immediately precedes the dawning of the light of Illumination. Without such wisdom and love filling Master Peter's being, he might instead have determined me to be unfit for the spiritual path.

God created us to be carriers of the power that heals bodies, hearts, and souls, and to be full of the peace that passes all understanding. We were also created to find such deep joy in coming into sync with the plan for our lives that, once we find it, nothing can ever take that joy from us. Finally, we were created to be able to develop into beings as bright and lifegiving as the sun in the sky, representing God on Earth.

Some people may be astonished to hear that we will be able to see God if we find a teacher to help us through the veil that separates us from God. This *is* the deepest desire of the soul. And nothing in life or in death can take its place. What great sadness for a soul to arrive at the time to leave this body permanently and find out that it missed the point of being on Earth altogether. To find out at that point what could have been, what potential was missed, is the deepest of sorrows. And such sadness is the experience of the vast majority of humankind when they die. Most never knew they had a choice to do otherwise. You now do. Can you feel that desire in your soul? Do you understand that nothing else will satisfy it but the actual seeing and knowing of God? What are you going to do about it?

You have the choice of seeking out a school that has master teachers capable of bringing you into this experience, or you can choose to wait for another time in this life, or another incarnation. God gives you the freedom to choose how long you wish to wait before you come to God.

No matter how much wisdom we may have come to in a previous lifetime, we enter into a new body without experience. As souls, we still have to begin being infants and learn how to use a body again. We have to learn to walk and talk, use the potty, and eat by ourselves. The soul has done this many times before, and that is why we can relearn it all so amazingly quickly. In fact, we are not learning these things, we are only remembering how to do them and getting our new little bodies to cooperate.

For the first seven years of life, we work on developing the use of the physical body. During the next seven years, from ages 7 through 14, we learn how to reason. From ages 14 to 21, we develop our emotional capacities. This is why teenagers often go through such intensely emotional times, and why others may find it so hard to be around them. From ages 21 until 28, we are meant to be working on our spiritual development. This does not mean that we are not working on all four aspects of development during the rest of our lives. Any part of our physical, rational, emotional, or spiritual side that missed development will continue to need work beyond age 28. If we somehow manage to do most of the work that was apportioned to each period in or around that period, then by age 28 we will be ready to seriously begin training for the purpose for which we were born. We will be ready to claim our rights as sons and daughters of God and enter into finding our missions and fulfilling them.

Because we do not have much experience as we enter each of the stages of development, we can often get into situations that are dangerous and could cost us our physical or emotional health, or even our lives. Sometimes extraordinary measures are needed to keep us from harm as we enter a new stage of development in which we have not had any previous experience. Each of us has spiritual guardians who will sometimes take on bodies, intervening in a situation that could throw us off track and away from our purpose. There is usually an otherworldly feeling to such interventions, which we sometimes don't recognize until the events are over. For me, the pattern became clearer over the years as I repeatedly experienced the intervention of two mysterious men who came to bail me out of dangerous situations or teach me lessons.

Teenage Recklessness and an Experience of Being Protected

I was 16 years old in 1970, and the era of the hippie generation was in full swing. I felt as though I had almost missed the revolution, as I was entering my mid-teens at the tail end of that period. I loved many things about the movement. I appreciated that the inner values of love and consciousness mattered so much more than material possessions and social status. I was delighted that the movement proclaimed that we are all in community and should share everything with each other. Being a teenager, I also relished the anti-authoritarian tone and the promotion of rebellion and acting out of all kinds, unless such actions could harm other people.

While experimenting with hallucinogenic drugs, I discovered an entirely different reality than the one I had previously known. When I was high on LSD, I found that I perceived, interpreted, and valued things from quite a different perspective. I began to question how we know which "reality" is real. What if the everyday reality we hold to be the true one is actually the illusion? What if a much greater reality existed that we have no idea about and which would entirely change our way of seeing and living? Along with taking mind-altering chemicals, I also began to read some of the counterculture's literature on consciousness, Eastern philosophy, and religion. I soon found that most of my hippie friends who were altering their minds by chemical means were not at all interested in the consciousness issues, but simply wanted to have fun. I enjoyed the fun aspect of altering my states of consciousness, too, but I always found myself wondering about the meaning and reality of what I experienced when in a drug-induced altered state, versus the meaning and reality of my normal states of consciousness. Still, I delved ever deeper into questioning all that I had held to be true, wanting to know how I could find an absolute Truth. Recreational drugs were a means of having experiences of other realms for a relatively short time, until I found my first spiritual practice when I was 19. In the meantime, it seemed to be the best method of exploration of consciousness that I could find. Later, when I discovered the uplift and enlargement of consciousness I could gain from meditation and spiritual practices, I never again wanted to cloud my mind and my being with chemicals. The spiritual highs proved to be much more satisfying and actually contributed to my growth, without fogging my awareness as the drugs had done.

I had an experience during this time that made me wonder if I was under someone's protection, if some being or beings were watching out for me. One day when I had spent all my bus money, yet needed to get home, I hitchhiked, which I did now and again. I made a rule for myself that I would never get in the backseat of a two-door car, nor would I ever get in a car that was occupied by two or more men. But on this particular day I broke both of those rules and got in the back seat of a two-door car with two men in the front seat. As soon as the car started moving, I began to wish I had waited for another ride. The two men were acting strange, with a mysterious air, and were talking back and forth in terms I could not catch but that seemed to refer to me. I began to get a sense that I had entered into a potentially bad situation and fear crept up my spine, making the hair on my arms stand on end. I told them that I had changed my mind and wanted to get out. They just told me "no," and that they would take me all the way.

I was in a cold sweat when they veered off of the main road and began heading for the woods. Terror that I would be brutally raped and/or beaten, and possibly killed, overcame me. I pleaded with them to let me out, telling them that I could walk from there. They laughed and continued on down an unpaved road deep into the woods. I cried, pleaded, and begged that they let me go and not hurt me. At the end of this dirt road, I could see nothing but trees for miles around us. They brought the car to a stop and turned off the engine. They both turned around in their seats and looked at me as I cried and pleaded, shaking with fear and dread. I thought my life was over and wondered what horrors they had in mind for me before they killed me. Glaring at me, one of them said threateningly, "We have got you now. You have no way out. We can do anything we want with you." I begged and pleaded and wailed some more.

Then the driver said, "How old are you?" I told them I was 15 and that I really wanted to go home.

He said angrily, "Do you understand how stupid you are to put yourself in such a situation? Do you see you are defenseless against us?" He then softened and said, "I have a daughter your age. I dread the thought that she would ever do anything as stupid as what you did here today!" I did not know what was happening. I stopped crying and studied their faces. Were they actually not intending to hurt me? What was going on?

The driver turned back around in his seat, started up the engine, and said, "We are taking you to your house. We want to speak to your parents. Surely they would want to know what a ridiculously stupid thing you did today. Where do you live?" I was just beginning to take in that I was going to live to see another day when the fear of them telling my parents set in. I begged them not to tell my parents. After insisting for a while, they said they would make me a deal. If I absolutely promised them that I would never hitchhike alone again, they would drop me off at my house and not come in to speak with my parents. As they drove me to my house they were muttering between themselves about how crazy young people are, how risk-taking, and how frightening the thought was to them of their daughters ever living so dangerously.

When I entered my house, I felt as if I had had an otherworldly experience. I was completely disoriented and sat for a long time trying to sort it all out. Something about the two men was so intense, and yet so protective and loving, that I did not know where to file the experience in my understanding. I knew I had been the recipient of a big dose of grace and that I had been protected from harm and taught a big lesson all at once. I was deeply grateful to God and never hitchhiked alone again. I also began to wonder for what purpose I might have been saved. Was I to contribute something that made it worth the while of these intense beings to intervene like they did to teach me to take better care of myself? How was it that I was so loved and protected? I certainly did not seem to deserve it, considering all the grief I was causing my parents as a drug-taking, lying, and unruly teenager. I also sensed that if I did not learn from this and continued to take great risks, I might not fare as well next time. Grace had intervened this time. Next time the decision of my divine guardians might be that I needed a painful experience to learn the lesson. How loving of them to first give me a chance to learn gently! I would take it to heart. I would value my life more, because maybe, in the end, I would have something to give back to humankind and to God.

3

LIFE ALONE: THE TIME BEFORE FINDING YOUR SPIRITUAL PATH

If a word of a great mystic…finds an echo in one or another of us, may it not be that there is a mystic dormant within us, merely waiting for an occasion to awake?

—Henri Bergson, *Creative Evolution*, 1907

The Sobering Effect of the Suicide of a Friend

I have said that the desire to find God is deeply imprinted on every soul. Yet, so few people choose to make the fulfillment of that desire a priority in their lives. Why are most people not conscious of the relevance or even the possibility of the quest to find God even though it is of such vital importance to their souls? Clearly, I had early stirrings of a spiritual nature; just as many, if not most, children will if they are introduced to a religious or spiritual practice that is at least relatively positive. I was fortunate to be introduced to the concept of an inner path through reading *Siddhartha*. But I still needed to grow up and enter the world of adulthood. I needed to learn about relationships, about intimacy and sexuality, about the working world, and about the existence of evil and ill will.

Once I turned 16, my parents felt even more helpless in knowing how to raise me and keep me from harm. When I was a junior in high school, I began to miss a lot of school while I hung out with hippie friends in the city. I was much more interested in the hippie life and romance than anything taking place in school. The only goal I had at the time was to move into a crash pad in Zurich where all the hippies stayed who had nowhere else to go. I imagined what a free and wonderful life that would be. I was full of idealism about sharing all our material goods, free love, and having no possessiveness about anything. "All you need is love" rang true in my heart. I had no interest in a career or ambitions for the future. I saw career ambitions (true to hippie ideals) to be traps of a capitalist society. Love was going to take over the world, and we, the hippies, were going to be the bearers of that truth. It was an exciting, and what proved to be a dangerous, time to be young and foolish.

I began dating a guy named Dieter who was a drug dealer. I thought the fact that he was a drug dealer was exciting. Being involved in that dangerous world made me feel more like an adult. He confided in me and showed me where he kept his stash of liquid LSD. One day he was arrested. I knew that he had two apartments, and his friends told me which one he had been arrested in. I knew the LSD was in the other apartment, and I knew where he hid a key. I was caught up in being a hero and saving Dieter from the bad police, who did not understand our revolution of consciousness and love. I went to the apartment, took the bottle of LSD, and brought it to a nice gentle hippie guy named Mark, who I knew had sold some of Dieter's goods before. I asked him to sell it and keep the money for Dieter when he got back.

Dieter got out of police custody about a week later. He immediately came looking for me, asking where the LSD was. I told him Mark had sold it and was holding the money for him. Instead of being grateful to me for having saved him from being caught with it, he became irate. He screamed and yelled that I had no business taking things into my own hands and that I would pay for this. I did not understand what had happened in my idealistic little land of love and peace. I was devastated. I also began to get a sense that Dieter was really an unsavory and potentially dangerous kind of a guy and that I was in way over my head. My parents seemed somehow to find out that I was in trouble. To my great surprise, my father abruptly announced that I was leaving for the USA the following Monday and was to live with my sister and her husband in Mississippi until my first college semester began. I had just finished my junior year in high school and had been accepted into an early admission program by a small Christian college in Liberty, Missouri. My parents probably hoped that I would be less bored with college than high school, and that maybe I would stay out of trouble.

When I arrived in the USA, I stayed with my sister and her husband for several weeks. My brother-in-law and I did not get along and I felt I could not tolerate staying with him and my sister any longer. I joined a traveling magazine sales team, and over the next two months I sold magazines door to door all over Mississippi, Alabama, Louisiana, and Georgia. One man loosed his dogs on me, a police chief tried to rape me, a couple of people pulled guns out when they came to the door that I was knocking on, and I was involved in chase scenes in which my magazine team and I were running away from dangerous people. It was a hardcore introduction to the "real" world. More of my innocence and idealism were shed. I simply tried to stay alive and safe. I prayed for protection and hoped God would come to my aid, even though I had not exactly been on best behavior over the last few years.

I had wanted for so long to be on my own in the world. But this was not what I had imagined. I thought people were for the most part kind, and that running free wherever I chose would be fun. Instead, I discovered that many people were uncaring or even mean. I found that there was actually very little love to be found in the hippie "free loving" ideal. Now the world looked scarier than I had imagined it to be. It was sad to lose all that idealism. I felt more vulnerable and less sure of myself, and of what might lay ahead for me in my life. God was, at this point, not a major part of my picture of life ahead. But the world without spirit was looking less rosy all the time. I did not know what I would do, or how I would find meaning, purpose, and a community of people who had ideals that I could share. I did not yet know that such a community would need to be a spiritual one, but I was realizing that communities based on hippie ideals only were not going to fulfill my hopes for shared meaning and conscious and caring relationships.

Nine months later, when I was back in Switzerland, I found out that my friend Mark had been arrested after Dieter reported to the police that Mark and I had robbed him. Mark was high on LSD when he was arrested and interrogated, and it was more than he could take. He had a psychological breakdown, and spent the next nine months in a mental health facility, serving his entire sentence there. During all his time in detainment, he thought that I had turned him in. It destroyed his faith in the goodness of people, and in his ability to know people. It was not until I bumped into him upon his release that I heard all this and set the story straight with him. But the emotional damage he had sustained in these months proved to be more than he could bear. Mark committed suicide a few weeks after I told him what had actually happened. When I heard of his death, I was overwhelmed with the feeling that he had taken the fall for me, that rightfully it should have been me who was incarcerated, not him. He had been in jail, and hence in the psychiatric ward, because I had asked him to do this favor. I had gotten off without a scratch. Now I had a life on my conscience. This was serious.

There were aspects of hippie life I still embraced. I was still interested in ecology and world peace, and in exploring alternative and consciousness-raising community lifestyles. But I had become wary of people and groups who were primarily associated with drugs, and I was not so sure I knew where I was going in life, nor was I certain that my life was going to turn out okay. But I was hopeful that I would find my way and somehow felt that I would be protected in my search.

The Life Tasks

As we make the transition from childhood to adolescence and then into adulthood, we enter perilous waters. Many young people sense that danger and become very cautious in their decision-making relating to relationships, fun, and work. They set goals and try to keep out of trouble, while sometimes envying the boldness of those who are not so cautious. For another group of young people, it never seems soon enough for them to get into adult activities. They take reckless chances as they step out into the unknown worlds of mind-altering substances, sexual encounters, relationships of various kinds—sometimes with questionable characters—and any other experiences they can find. As a teenager, I fit into this latter category of youths. There is an in-between group that takes some chances and also exerts caution, is somewhat loose and free flowing with their life plans, but holds onto goals and limits of how far they will venture from the well-trodden path that their parents and mentors took. I was not one of those. My willingness to take risks got me into some dangerous situations, including the hitchhiking experience and the attempt to save my drug-dealing boyfriend from being arrested. But it was that same willingness to go out on a limb that enabled me to doggedly search for a path to God, no matter where this search led me. I was willing to go anywhere and do anything within ethical limits, in order to come into a deep face-to-face relationship with God. The character trait of courage to do many things was therefore essential to what was to be my path to enlightenment. But there were other life tasks I yet had to address before I was to find my way to a teacher and to the inner path.

Life does, in fact, present each of us with a series of tasks that we must learn to master. These tasks can become so all-consuming that people forget the task for which they incarnated: to find the God in the center of their being and get in tune with their individual life purposes. That divinely spiritual task can become lost in the shuffle of the daily tasks of Earth life. What are those earthly tasks, and what are we supposed to gain from each?

Task One: Leaving the Parents' House

One of the first and most important adult tasks is to separate from the parents and launch out into the world. When children successfully accomplish this task, they will find that they have freedom in their thinking and feeling to move in whatever direction they choose. I was fiercely determined from early childhood to make my parents understand that they should never try to get in the way of my freedom to do whatever I decided to do. This made their job of raising me quite challenging, but they did completely let go of trying to control me by the time I was 17. They entrusted me to God's care and my own common sense. Sometimes parents and other relatives do as my parents did, and have helped freethinking and feeling occur by raising their sons and daughters to think for themselves and have faith in their own decision-making abilities. However, sometimes a person has to arrive at that independence in the face of intense resistance from his or her family. Many parents hold onto their adult children under the guise of love. They often emotionally cripple their offspring and prevent them from living fulfilled lives. A truly healthy parent-child relationship would consist of parents who are happy in their own lives and their own endeavors and are self-reliant in fulfilling their own needs and dreams. Healthy parents believe in their children's ability and right to make their own life choices and support them in doing so. Family members can enjoy contact with each other without emotional dependency or demands for loyalty to family ideas, patterns, and values.

The inability to enter into a state of either peaceful or, if necessary, adversarial mental and emotional independence from the parents is one of the primary reasons many people cannot follow a committed spiritual path. The mystical path is a rare choice for a person to make. Most people do not feel motivated to make the finding and developing of the inner relationship with God the most important aspect of their lives. When a family member announces that he or she has embarked on such a journey, his or her relatives will usually have no idea what that announcement means. Most families want their children to follow the family tradition regarding religion and will offer up moderate or even severe messages of disapproval to the children who choose otherwise. Many adults cannot find the courage to stand up to their family's resistance to a nonconforming spiritual path, and will discontinue any form of development that disturbs the family dynamic. If adult children have not gained emotional and intellectual independence from the family, their parents' arguments, concerns, and appeals to family tradition and values may also sway them. Because I established my absolute right to such independence from my family at a very young age, my family accepted that right

and rarely even voiced opinions about my choice of lifestyle and spiritual practices, even when I know my choices were most strange and probably even disturbing to them. They knew I was not interested in hearing any input that was
negative, and they accepted the boundaries I set.

When adult children allow the parents' opinions, concerns, and appeals to
family tradition to sway them from the spiritual path they wanted to pursue, the
parents still hold the place of God in those adult children's lives. For them, the
family of origin and the parents are those whom one must listen to, please, and
obey. They are the ones one must love above all. These individuals will remain
children all their lives. They will not be able to enter fully into union with a
spouse because the primary place in their hearts is still held by the parents. Their
children will have to be raised at least partially by the grandparents' standards.
And God will have to remain the God of their ancestors, off in a faraway place,
approached or not approached by whatever means the tradition requires.

The task of separating from the family of origin does not need to be completed before one begins the spiritual path, but the aspirant will need to be ready
to make the potentially unpopular decision of beginning such a path. The rest of
the work of coming into an autonomous and free inner and outer relationship
with relatives can, and usually does, continue to develop in the early stages of the
spiritual path.

Task Two: Establishing a Means of Livelihood

As we enter the adult world, most of us need to take on the task of making a livelihood. From the spiritual perspective, the purposes of doing work in the world
are:

1.   To contribute something useful to society. In return we are able to sus-
     tain ourselves, thereby doing our fair share and not being a burden to
     anyone else.

2.   To develop the skillful use and integration of body, mind, and/or heart.

3.   To create contacts with different people, often from different back-
     grounds, so that we can expand our experience and knowledge of peo-
     ple.

4.   To learn to work in different relationships with people, where some-
     times we are the underlings and sometimes the boss. Through these

roles we find out how to learn and how to teach, how to be strong and solid, and how to be soft and kind.

5.   To learn to be disciplined, consistent, and responsible, both daily and over the long-term.

Notice that, from your soul's perspective, your livelihood is not meant to be a means for you to gain power and influence over others. Nor is it a means to accumulate immense amounts of material goods, at the expense of nurturing other aspects of your being and life in the world. Your livelihood is also not meant to serve as your reason to be alive or your definition of who you are and what your value is. An ideal means for making a living would give a person enjoyment in a line of work, plenty of opportunity for growth and development, and some means by which he or she could develop communication and relational skills. It should provide enough money so that the person does not have to be worried about making ends meet. Work should not take so much time out of a person's life that other aspects suffer.

When work and money, or the lack of it, take too much of our attention, we may find that we lose our connection with the need to establish a deep spiritual life. We fall prey to the illusion that we don't have enough time for our soul's work and that a spiritual life would be a luxury. We make spiritual development one of the items on our list of things we need to get to someday, and then often never get around to it. Many people come to the end of their days on Earth and discover that they spent way too much time on what mattered least: making money. It is sad and yet so common.

My own willingness to take risks allowed me to be open to many different ways of making a living. Though I was to primarily earn money through work I loved doing, such as midwifery, social service provision, and psychotherapy, I never hesitated to take various odd jobs along the way when I was between times during which I could live off of my primary professions. I learned much through these varied employments, and have applied the resulting skills throughout my life. I never thought that work mattered more than my spiritual life, and I stayed doggedly determined to never let it get in the way of my spiritual training, growth, and later my service to others. Where then was a partner to fit into my priorities? I held the spiritual path first; making a living followed along further down my list of priorities. How about a mate? How would he fit into my life?

Task Three: Finding, Catching, and Keeping a Mate

The task of finding suitable mates, entering into committed relationships with them, and maintaining those relationships in good working order is once again a task that a great number of people allow to get in the way of their path to God. Finding a loving mate with whom to share one's life is undeniably a very important part of being human and a deep-seated desire within most people. Long-term shared commitments allow us to grow and develop ourselves in many ways that would be difficult through any other means. Virtually no other task in life is as challenging, and virtually no other task is potentially more rewarding or more apt to tear us apart emotionally, leaving us feeling devastated and bereft.

The great need and longing for a mate that most people feel actually originates within the soul. We know on a soul level that we have the possibility of finding unconditional love that will heal us and fill us with peace and joy. We know this to be a major life task. What we don't know is that the desired relationship will only be possible within ourselves. No human love will ever be truly unconditional and perfect. No human love will ever fulfill all our needs. No human love will ever be infallible and eternal. However, the love relationship between the soul and the God-Self can be all those things. This is what is programmed into our souls before we are born, but we get confused and look for such love outside of ourselves.

A mate is supposed to be one who walks with us and beside us. Sometimes we share spiritual paths with our partners, and that can be truly wonderful. But when we stand before God, we are, in fact, always alone. The God in the center of our beings is who we need to come into relationship with, as our mate needs to do with the God at the center of his or her being. Only there will we find the deep, great joy of perfect love and perfect peace. The human counterpart will always fall short of that ideal. The trap that people fall into with this life task of finding and joining with a mate is that they often make their mate the god in their lives. Usually this lasts until children are born or other interests supersede, at which time the new distraction becomes the most precious and worshipped object of the person's attention and affection.

In addition to the misplacement of god-like expectations onto our mate, there is another trap related to one's partner to which women are especially vulnerable. Many women tell me that they are waiting to begin a spiritual path because they want their husband to walk that path with them. Or, they say they simply cannot have a spiritual practice because he would not approve. In my experience, men are often hesitant to join a group or ask for spiritual instruction, and they do not usually get caught up in their wives' need for companionship in such ventures. In fact, some men would prefer to take up their own spiritual paths. This is not, of course, the case with all women or all men, but it does seem to be a common pattern.

It is an error to await the presence of one's spouse before beginning spiritual training. You must realize that the spiritual path is between your soul and God, not between you and your spouse. The path is, in fact, more important than anything else on Earth, including the spouse. Trying to push one's spouse into a spiritual practice is also inappropriate and disrespectful of his right to decide for himself when he wants to take on what spiritual practice, if at all. Besides, it won't work. In fact, the reluctant partner may move farther away from seeking God if he or she feels pushed. We must each give our mates total and complete freedom to search or not to search for God in whatever way they feel moved to do so. We also have every right to expect them to give us the same liberty to choose for ourselves. God gives us this freedom, and we should give the same to each other. You cannot, therefore, ask your partner to enter upon a path for you. You can, however, expect and stand on your right to have your partner support your choice of whatever path you feel moved to travel upon.

What about those who do not find a suitable mate with whom to have a long-term relationship? They often fall into the trap of expending most of their energy either looking for or avoiding committing to a partner. This search-and-possess or play-with-but-don't-commit-to mission becomes the god in their lives. These folks often never lift their heads out of the ups and downs of their love-lives long enough to even look for the most fulfilling possibility. If those who are single could find a freedom from the obsession with finding or avoiding a mate and simply focus on the other life tasks and on finding God, they would either find a mate over time or discover what a blessing it can be to be single and therefore mobile and flexible. Being alone allows one to be available for many possible life adventures and changes that might not have been possible with a mate. A single person does not have the complications of trying to work out a combined, or at least supported, agreement of how they will live their spiritual lives within the relationship and home. That freedom can be a great blessing.

I have enjoyed a long marriage followed by a celibate life that I began when I was 45. The freedom afforded me through being celibate has opened up so many opportunities to fulfill my life's work and allowed me to discover the quiet joy of solitude. I am grateful for being given the opportunity to experience both states of being married and being celibate, and finding the different blessings inherent in each.

Task Four: Raising a Family

The fourth major life task given to humans is the decision whether to have and raise children. Some people have strong feelings about wanting to raise or not raise children from early on in their lives. Some people stay neutral to the subject until much later in their childbearing years. Not everyone needs to be raising children and, according to recent statistics, one out of four Americans will not raise children during this life. Those who never have the opportunity to raise children or who choose not to can often have meaningful relationships with someone else's children if they want to. This can be very fulfilling for all involved parties. Other people may choose to spend their adult lives almost entirely in the company of other adults. This can also be a fulfilling life, and for some kinds of life work and callings, it can be the most conducive and expedient way to live. Many an important work generated by a group or by individuals would not be possible without the help of those who are not tied down by family and children. It can be a great gift to the world to forego those pleasures and commitments, either by choice or by circumstance, and be fully available to the work one is called to do. Often the work itself then becomes like a child to that person, and the joy of seeing its growth and development can be similar to that of raising a child.

Those people who do end up raising children tend to find that there are few things in life that are as challenging and as rewarding. Bearing and caring for children will stretch a person to new dimensions of giving by having someone else's needs supersede one's own day after day. Though one can get very attached to a spouse, the attachment to one's children is often much stronger and longer lasting. Because of the attachment, this task can be another major trap that can keep people away from the life-purpose of their souls. In case you have forgotten, the life purpose of every soul is to find God at its center and to come into its purpose for being on Earth. How easily we forget this truth.

As wonderful, difficult, gratifying, and all-consuming as raising children can feel, it is yet still meant to be a life task through which one passes. It is not meant to be the purpose for which one lives. Nor is it meant to be a parent's source of meaning and their primary contribution to the earth. When a parent makes children the center of his or her universe, they have put them in the place of God in their lives. This tends to have a negative effect on the marriage, as well as on the given parent's continued development within his or her own psyche and spirit. Then, when the children grow up and leave home, the parents often realize their relationship was entirely centered on the children, and they no longer know each other. The same holds true for them knowing themselves. Often they will try to hold onto the grown children and control them through guilt or bribes. These become the adult children who have a lot of trouble separating from their families and living fulfilling, self-directed lives as independent adults.

If this, the fourth major life task, can be accomplished without losing oneself in it, then a person will be in very good shape for entering upon the spiritual path. His or her family will be greatly blessed. But don't take it lightly: All of society will rally against the ones who do this. This is because the true religion of American society is that one should love one's children above all else, and should serve only them. America's second most important belief is that romantic love is the other noblest purpose for living. Those who fulfill these two dictums of our society are considered by the vast majority of people to be veritably "good." If they, in addition, have also developed successful careers and have maintained loyalty to their families of origin, most everyone would agree that such people have indeed succeeded in life.

Do you see how these priorities are the opposite of what the soul asks of us? God said in the Old Testament that a man should leave his parents and home and cling to his wife. He was not told to hang onto the parents, but to separate from them. Jesus said that unless a person loves God more than spouse or children or parents or possessions, that person is not worthy of the kingdom of heaven. Jesus also said that to love God with all your heart and mind and soul is the most important commandment. To love your neighbor as yourself is the second. How do these go along with our society's views? Not too well. You can see why a person who chooses to make the search for God and being in God's service central to their lives, above the love of spouse and children, above the pursuit of career and riches, above loyalty to parents and family tradition, will often be viewed unfavorably by our society.

Why is it so hard to remember the purpose for which we came to earth, if it is written on our souls, and it is our souls' greatest desire? The traps are very hard to evade, and our society's guidelines run counter to those of God. Travelers through life who truly want to go where their souls lead them will need much courage and perseverance. They will need to get in touch with that burning desire within them and make a commitment to follow it. They will need to follow the great teachers' directives concerning what matters most, not their families' or their societies'. If they can jump these hurdles and keep sight of the goal and their commitment to it, then at some point the angels will look down and say, "Look at that one! Someday that one may become a great servant of God!"

College, Marriage, and the Birth and Death of a Baby

My first semester at college was difficult because I was still not quite used to living in the United States. The social norms that others took for granted stumped me. I was only 16 years old and was lacking in self-discipline and focus. I intended to major in political science, as I still had the same need I had at age five to help make the world a better place. An Italian man whom I had been dating for the several weeks before I left Switzerland wrote me a letter saying that he wanted me to come back. I quickly sold most of my possessions and left for Italy. The letter was in Italian, which I tried to decipher via my knowledge of Latin and French. It turned out he had actually been suggesting that our letter writing was useless because we probably would not see each other again. This man, Sal, was to become my husband five months later. At age 17, having left my family of origin (the first adult life task), I was determinedly tackling two more tasks. I married, and gave birth to my first child before I was 18. None of Sal's and my friends were marrying and having children at this young age. But something inside us pushed us to forge ahead. Many years later, I came to understand that we needed to move quickly into the childbearing and child-raising years, because we were not to have very long together. Twenty-eight years later, just as our youngest child graduated from high school, Sal went back to Italy to spend his last year there. He died of heart disease at the age of 53. I was 46 and received guidance from the God-Self that I was to convert our house into a training center for spiritual development and dedicate myself full-time to this work. We spent exactly enough years together to raise the children, and then each of us went on to our next steps. At the early ages of 17 and 23, our souls seemed to know that our time would be limited and we needed to get going.

Sal and I set up household in Pompeii, Italy. During my pregnancy, I was misdiagnosed with a liver disease and received two injections a day. About six weeks before I was due, an injection site got infected. The infection spread throughout my body and the ensuing fever initiated premature labor. Our son Ian was born weighing four and a half pounds, and doing well considering his premature arrival. But the hospital's incubators were not functioning, so he was left with only hot water bottles to warm him. After eight hours, he was transported to another hospital that had an available incubator. He died four days later of pneumonia. No one was with him when he left his little body behind. He died alone in a machine, without Sal or I ever having held him. This was to be a quiet but deep sorrow for me until I reached a resolution with it a number of years later.

After giving birth to Ian, I was extremely ill with sepsis. My doctor asked Sal not to tell me that Ian had died because he was afraid that my condition was too fragile for such news. Sal had to come see me each day and pretended he had been to see Ian and that Ian was okay. I knew Ian was not well, but I did not know he had died. Ten days after I gave birth, my mother-in-law asked an English-speaking doctor who was not my own doctor to speak with me, as I was so sad. In English, the doctor asked me what church I belonged to. Surprised by his question, I reluctantly told him I had been raised a Baptist. He said, "There is a Baptist church not far from here. Go and confess your sins, and maybe your next baby will live." He walked out of the room. I gathered two things from what he said: that Ian had died and that it was my fault. The effect of these two pronouncements on my already weak body was more than my heart could take. I went into shock and my heart stopped beating. It felt to me like I stepped several inches back from my body and from my emotions. In that state I had no emotions. I was still looking out through my eyes, but in an emotionally detached way.

I don't know what I looked like, but when my mother-in-law saw me she ran out into the hall screaming for help. The doctor whose statements caused my heart to stop never turned around. He kept walking down the hall. My own doctor came running with a team and called the Italian equivalent of a "code blue." When injections into my heart muscle did not restart my heart, the doctor, convinced that I could hear him and could decide to come back if I chose, feverishly presented one reason after another why I should want to live. He told me Sal would miss me terribly; he told me I could have other children, that my parents would be so sad; he told me that I was young and would be healthy again. I considered each argument he offered. I felt myself standing between life and death, and I knew I could choose which way to go. None of the doctor's arguments changed my mind, and I felt paralysis creeping over me; blood was no longer circulating through my arteries and veins.

The doctor then told me that it was crazy for me to die just because of something a stupid doctor said to me. *This* was something I *did* consider. My doctor saw some response in me and frantically tried to recall what he had just said. As he remembered, he began to say over and over what a stupid jackass that other doctor was and how it was certainly crazy for anyone to die because of anything he might have said. As I got angry at the thought of the meanness of what the first doctor had said, my heart began to beat again. Why *should* I die because that doctor was mean and stupid? What did *he* know about me anyway? My blood started to circulate through my body, and the feeling of paralysis slowly faded away. My doctor knelt down beside the bed with sweat still covering his face from the effort he had expended trying to talk me back into life. He thanked God that I had not died.

Many times since then I have asked doctors whether they have ever heard of someone treating a shock-induced cardiac arrest as this man did. I have not found one. Somehow, I seemed to have been given one of the very few doctors of western medicine who understood that the soul has the power of decision over life and death. He believed that in a situation such as mine, one could address the soul directly and make a case to that soul for continued life. As he first began speaking with me, he told me that he could do nothing else for me medically, but that he believed I could hear him. In my open-eyed stare, he saw life and applied himself with everything he had to convincing me to choose life. *That* was truly a holistic doctor! I still bless him each time I think of him, and I thank God for him.

We are, in fact, always making choices in favor of life or of death. With the news of Ian's death, I nearly made a dramatic decision to exit from this life without further consideration. Usually our decisions would not bear such quick results. More often they will slowly, over time, lead us toward life or death. This applies to our physical as well as our emotional, mental, or spiritual deaths. Once we become aware that we are choosing life or death in many ways, throughout our time on earth we can decide to choose more consciously. The doctor who talked me back into life knew I had a choice. I now speak daily with people about the choice they have to live or die on all levels. Thanks to this wise physician, I am here to testify to the reality of our power to choose and the joy of choosing life.

4

YOGA, SUFISM, AND MYSTICAL CHRISTIANITY: FINDING A TRUE INNER PATH

Ask, and it will be given to you
Seek, and you will find
Knock and it will be opened to you.

—Jesus, *Matthew 7:7*

Astrology, Meditation, and Living in a Yoga Ashram

After my first-born son Ian died, and I recovered from my illness, I immediately became pregnant again. Once Sal and I realized I was pregnant, we knew that we did not want to go through another pregnancy and birth in Italy. We had discovered that the healthcare was far from adequate, and we were too afraid of experiencing another loss. We decided to move to the United States. My parents were living in Louisville, Kentucky, and they offered to help us get started if we came to live there. In June of 1972, we took our few belongings and moved to Louisville. Sal did not speak English, yet he adjusted quickly. Within a few months, he had a job, we were settled into a house, and I gave birth to our oldest daughter, Odessa. We were still somewhat shell-shocked from Ian's death. It took us a little while to trust that Odessa was here to stay; but soon her robust hold on life became so obvious that we relaxed into parenthood. I was 18 years old. The trauma of having lost Ian was so deep, and yet I had to go on, as I now had Odessa. I discovered I was strong, and that we humans seem to be able to hold up to much more than we imagine that we could. I did not know what to make of

Ian's birth and death, so I immersed myself in the joy of having a healthy baby, and let the rest go.

My parents received a three-year missionary assignment to India and had to leave a few weeks before Odessa was born. Odessa was three years old before they met her. My family always taught me that if God calls us to relocate in order to serve in another place, then we should go, regardless of attachments. I was, therefore, not sad about their leaving. Their departure also gave us the space we needed to grow into independent adulthood and make our own way. I managed real estate and stayed home with Odessa. Soon after our arrival in Louisville, I met a woman who was very involved with astrology. She interpreted everything a person did according to their sun sign. I thought she was crazy to be thinking this way, but I did not know enough about it to be able to argue it with her.

I came across a free introductory class in astrology and went with the intention of finding the evidence I needed to debunk her belief in this ancient science. I made a pest of myself in the class by questioning everything the instructor said. I did not have a religious objection to astrology. I simply could not understand how the position of the planets relative to where and when we are born could possibly have anything to do with our personalities and lives. Finally, exasperated by my disruptions, the instructor, whose name was Paul, asked me where I was born, on what date and what time of day. He opened a book called an Ephemeris, which lists all the planetary positions on any given date, and he quickly drew my basic astrological chart on the blackboard.

Paul then stood back, pondered the chart, and turned and described both of my parents to me based on my birth chart. His description was so accurate that it had the desired effect on me: I was speechless. I did not say another word for the rest of the class. In my mind, I rolled over and over what had happened, how it could have happened, and what it could mean. When the class ended, I went to Paul and said, "If this actually works, *why* does it work?" "To know *that*," he said, "you will have to come to my meditation class." I was even more speechless. What did he mean? Why would a meditation class tell me the basis for the truth of astrology? Now my curiosity was fired up, and I had to know more. I had an inner sense that I was drawing close to something that was of vital importance to me, as a being. This excited me, though I did not yet know how any of this could relate to the larger picture of me and my life on earth.

During my first meditation class, I slipped into a deep meditation and I found myself in the midst of two dramatic scenes; in each one I was a different person. In one I was an old woman whose husband had recently died. In the other I was a man, and I was swimming in the ocean with dolphins. When I came back to regular consciousness, I asked Paul about my experience. He listened carefully and said that I might have come upon past-life memories that were so close to the surface of my consciousness that it only took a little meditation for them to arise. "Past life memories?" I thought. And what is the truth and substance behind *that*? I began to get a sense that a complex and multifaceted world was opening before me, and that it might take me more than a class or two to understand what I had stumbled upon. I felt eager to enter into this unknown world, and sensed a deep-down knowledge that this all mattered much more than I could currently fathom.

Over the following months I read book after book about meditation, astrology, and reincarnation. These led me to read about yoga and the Eastern paths of spiritual development. The more I read, the hungrier I got for this food that I hoped would feed my heart, mind, body, and soul. This felt like what I had once, as a teenager, intuited to be somewhere "out there." It was as if my soul was jumping up and down inside of me shouting, "Yes! Yes! Yes!" I took yoga classes, but I did not want only the physical aspect of yoga. I wanted the spiritual development that I heard was available through the yogic traditions. I was 19 years old when I convinced Sal that we should move into a yoga ashram near where we lived and begin to live this life in all seriousness. Sal was not involved in the yogic practices, but he was willing to live there with me so that I could practice fully. I was now meditating and doing yogic asanas (postures) twice a day. I ate a very carefully proscribed vegetarian diet given to us by the head teachers of this yoga society, which included fasting one day every week. I bathed in certain ritual ways, wore the clothes that were recommended, and became disciplined in all the ways of this spiritual practice. The fasting was hard at first. I thought I could not live without food for a whole day. But before too long I got so accustomed to fasting once a week that I did not even feel hungry on the fast days. Focusing during meditation was also challenging. My mind wanted to wander and my emotions seemed to be calling me to follow them into every large or small issue that might get a rise out of me, drawing me away from my intention of focusing inside myself, and being still. I found out that it took time and a lot of work to develop discipline. But my desire to grow spiritually was so great that I was willing to wage war against my resistance to disciplining my body and mind, and work to attain control over both. I discovered that this was a slow process, and patience with myself was to be one of the byproducts of learning to meditate.

After living in this spiritual environment for several months, the day I had been awaiting arrived. One of the yogis from India, who was empowered by and represented the guru of our yogic association, came around to meet with all the members individually. This was a once-a-year occasion, and I was very excited about it. When I met with the teacher, we sat in meditation. He gave me a mantra and then instructed me on how to use it. A mantra is a spiritual word or phrase that is repeated over and over and is meant to form a spiritual backdrop to all of one's thinking and feeling processes. The teacher gave me a Sanskrit mantra that meant, "I am He." It was to be a constant reminder that I am the God within me. I was also given a Sanskrit name, which I used from that day on. The entire following year, I worked diligently with my meditations and my mantra. I had no idea how this mantra related to me and what I was to grow into spiritually. I did, however, faithfully work with it, hoping it was having some kind of beneficial effect, even without my understanding it. I could hardly wait for the year to pass so I could see the teacher again. I was hoping that he would help me move on to the next step.

When the year was up, the teacher returned. I told him that I had faithfully done all of the practices and was hoping he would give me the next step. The teacher became somewhat incensed with me. He asked me what made me think I was ready for another step. I told him that I had no idea where I was on the path, but I knew that I wanted to go as far as I could in this lifetime and that I would do whatever it took to progress. If I was in spiritual kindergarten, then I would like to know what I needed to do to progress to first grade. If I was in fifth grade, I would like to be shown how to progress to sixth grade. The yogi was not at all happy with me. He scolded me, saying that I was arrogant to think that I was to progress spiritually, and that such growth was not possible for everyone. He told me to continue the spiritual exercise he had given me for another year.

I was perplexed. I searched my heart and mind to see if I felt I was arrogant in wanting to progress spiritually. I simply wanted to grow, and I could not see how that could be wrong. I did not feel presumptuous, since I did not presume to be any particular place on the path. I was willing to do whatever work was needed to move along. What was I to do? Maybe another year of being very diligent with my practices would bring me to the place I needed to be for the teacher to give me more. So I settled into applying myself even more to all the spiritual practices given to me through this yogic path. I looked forward to the return of the teacher the following year with great hope and anticipation. When the teacher came and I met with him, he was still quite irked at my request to move ahead on the path. He told me once again that I was being arrogant and to continue with the same practices for another year. I felt heart-broken and quite discouraged.

I was now 22 years old and had two children, Odessa and Nathan. Sal and I had decided to give birth to Nathan at home. Because there was no one in the area who would attend to us at home, we bought some books about home birth, learned all we could, and prepared to have an unattended home birth. Our plan was to stay home as long as everything was progressing perfectly, and to go to the hospital if anything unusual happened. My labor with Odessa had been smooth, lasting only three hours, and I believed I would likely have the same kind of labor again. We called an ambulance to stand by while the actual delivery was happening. Nathan was born into Sal's hands without complications and, unbeknownst to us at the time, this event started the home-birth movement for Louisville and the surrounding areas! Other families began to ask me to help them have home births. I got training and certification to teach childbirth classes for do-it-yourself home births. Many of the families I taught invited me to come to their deliveries, and before I knew it I was receiving on-the-job training to be a midwife.

My work with childbearing families was exciting and in many ways fulfilling, yet I knew it was not my spiritual path. Practicing midwifery was a contribution I could make, and one I loved to do, and it had the added benefit of being a potential means to make a living. Midwifery was, however, not a path to God. I never confused my passion for helping childbearing women have good birth experiences with my search for a spiritual path that could bring me into a direct relationship with God. I felt passionate about both, and yet always knew that if I could choose to fulfill only one of those two passions, I would choose to find God, because I sensed that I would never feel complete until I did.

The Search for a Spiritual Path

What is a true spiritual path? How would you know if a given path you find is the right one for you? Many people have, as I did, a particular bias for or against a certain type of spiritual path. Some want something that is somewhat exotic and as far as possible from their parents' religions. Others want something that is within their family's religious tradition. Still others are open to anything except a certain path. Most people have no idea what they will be doing on a spiritual path once they find one. Fantasies proliferate within our minds when we do not yet have any experience from which to get a more concrete understanding. In my own fantasy of my spiritual path, I saw myself most likely in robes of white or orange, as I had seen the eastern gurus wear. My spiritual self-image ruled out any practice that was even remotely Christian. I envisioned myself becoming a quiet, holy being who virtually floated above the earth, dropping words of wisdom from the far beyond on all who entered into my glowing energy field.

In a broader sense, one might say that the preparation for the spiritual path begins at birth. From birth onward we have a series of experiences that form the foundation upon which we build our search for God. The order and school I now co-direct and in which I teach is called The Order of Christ/Sophia. When the students in this mystical training school make their first commitment and prepare to receive the first initiation, we have them look back on their lives and see how everything that previously happened prepared them to enter upon the path. It is very moving to see one's life from this perspective. It becomes quite clear how purposeful everything was: The type of family one was born into; the wounding one received as a child; the young adult experiences; one's friendships and intimate relationships; and one's religious background (or lack thereof). Everything serves as preparation so that we might find our way home to God within.

Life itself is a school. Before incarnating, we choose what lessons we need to learn during this life and what experiences will best prepare us to fulfill our mission. Being loved, supported, and validated by family and others teaches us to be confident, trusting, and open to love. Being abused, neglected, and invalidated also has a positive side. It teaches us to depend on ourselves, be cautious, and carefully choose the people with whom we enter into close relationships, making sure they are willing and able to be respectful and loving toward us. We can learn many other things from the painful experiences, such as how to overcome anger and rage, fear and mistrust, or pain and sadness. We, in fact, seem to learn more intensely from our painful experiences than from our pleasant ones. We can learn why we should not hurt others, how to break unhealthy family patterns, and how to survive and even thrive after being deeply wounded.

I call the life one has led before entering upon a spiritual path "the school of life." Different people have attended different schools of life. Therefore, what they bring to the path are different gifts and different issues. Any true spiritual path will be equipped to help people use their gifts and work through their issues. Most spiritual training of various kinds has ignored the emotional and psychological issues people carry with them. The students simply become "spiritual," hoping that they will be God-like without having to look at their wounds and their destructive habits. We in the Western world now know too much to continue to pretend that ignoring our problems works. We also have, more than ever before, an understanding of how to recognize and help heal people's wounds and shortcomings. A strong inner path needs not only be able to guide people into spiritual practices, but also needs to have instructors and guides who are psychologically sophisticated and who can help the students become whole throughout their beings.

Often, as Westerners, we are attracted to the Eastern inner paths. The Eastern paths have a reputation and time-tested methods for leading people within, and of transforming regular people into holy people. In fact, most westerners are not aware that Western mystical and esoteric paths exist. Buddhism and Hinduism are the most well-known ways. People have heard of Zen and yogis, but don't think of saints of the Christian path or Hasidic masters of the Jewish path as being of a similar stripe. And even if we know that inner teachings are available within our own religious tradition, many of us feel so overdosed and burnt out by the religion our parents imposed on us that we want something different. Some people initially had, as children, a very deep faith and hope in their religion and in God but became deeply disillusioned and hurt by a specific event that happened or, as they became older, by their own thinking and reasoning. Others never experienced anything of value within their religions and therefore lost hope of finding anything real flowing through that channel.

An interesting phenomena occurs within many people who, though wanting to have nothing to do with the religion of their families, still maintain family loyalty *against* certain other religions or denominations. Often it would be more acceptable to their family for them to practice a spirituality from a remote culture than to practice something much closer to home, against which there has been a long-held family bias. These biases are inculcated into the offspring with an amazing rate of success. Adult children who have disowned and separated themselves from almost everything their families taught about religion will often be loyal to the family prohibition—or even hatred against—another religion or faith. When a family has handed down such a teaching of discrimination against another faith, a member of that family who wishes to have the freedom to choose whichever inner path is right for him or her will need to come face to face with his or her family's issues. He or she will also need to be willing to risk the wrath of the family members for his or her perceived disloyalty.

The task of helping us get to *our* right path is up to our soul. Sometimes, however, our minds and emotions are not very happy with the path to which our soul seems to have led us. We may have imagined a certain brand of spiritual path, or one that would look from the outside a particular way, and instead we find ourselves coming across a path that is of the variety that we have decided we disdain. This was my experience. One could use a metaphor of having prayed and prayed for ice cream. Finally—miraculously—ice cream becomes available. Then we say: "But I didn't want chocolate ice cream! I wanted vanilla!" We begged for ice cream, and now we are complaining about the flavor we have been given. My bias was entirely against any Christian path or practice, and yet that was precisely where my journey was to lead me. In the end, only the mystical Christian path would take me where I had hoped the eastern paths would lead.

First Encounter with a Mystical Christian Order

Not long after the teacher met with me for the second time at the yoga ashram and once again told me to do the same exercises for another year, one of my housemates informed me that down the street from us, a new spiritual center had opened. He said that the center seemed to be teaching some alternative Christian practice. My answer was swift: "I am not interested in anything Christian." "Why not?" he asked. I told him that I'd had Christianity imposed on me since birth, and that I needed a real path, not another nice church. He told me that three or four women ran the place and taught classes in mystical Christianity. He asked me if I would come with him to check it out. I grudgingly agreed. The class turned out to be very small. During the first half, the instructor cited a passage from the Bible and asked us what we understood it to mean on an interior level. I didn't know what she was asking. She explained that Jesus taught on several different levels. One of the ways to examine His teachings and the story of His life is to look at all the characters in the story as parts of ourselves. A part of us doubts like Thomas, but through our doubts, asks for firsthand experience, receives it, and becomes a knower of Truth. Part of us betrays the God within us, as did Judas. Another part can love immensely and be transformed, like Mary Magdalene. Still another part is pure and desires only God, and can conceive and give birth to the Christ within us, like Mother Mary did. And part of us originates from God, and is truly the son/daughter of God within us, as Jesus was.

I had intensely guarded myself against liking anything that was Christian or from the Bible. But the material that this woman was teaching fascinated me. After giving us the examples of what some of the characters in the Bible might represent inside of us, the teacher went back to asking what this story could be telling us about aspects of ourselves. Applying these examples, new insights opened up before my mind's eye. I was intrigued. The instructor used the second hour of the class to teach inner esoteric and mystical teachings about humans, God, and creation. At the end of the class, she led us through a spiritual exercise that left me feeling sky-high. And what was that light I saw in this instructor's eyes? I kept trying to look more closely to see whether it was the room light bouncing off her pupils. Another vowed Sister (which is what I now knew they were) came in after class, and I saw the same kind of light in her eyes. The energy they carried was the energy I wanted to develop at the ashram but knew was not yet present there. I went home perplexed, disturbed, and slightly intrigued.

Back at the ashram, I had much to contend with inside my own head and heart. I could not deny that I had had both the scriptures and my own inner workings elucidated through the Bible class. I could not deny that the class on the cosmology of all and everything was fascinating. And I could not deny that the spiritual exercise caused me to be in an elevated state for hours. I was also quite clear that I did not want to get involved in anything Christian. My husband was interested in Sufi work. I could do that. I had my yogic training. I could do that. I had heard a bit about mystical Judaism. I could do that. But *not* Christianity! I had ranted and raved against it for so long. It would be embarrassing to be a Christian. What would my friends say? And worse than that, what if my parents gloated at being right, after I had finally convinced them to accept the rightness of my yogic path?

No, I was not going to do anything more than go back to a couple more classes, to try to understand how they did things there. Maybe I could learn something that we could apply at the ashram.

So I was back at class the following week. A different Sister taught. When I asked why they were called Sisters, she told me that they had taken life vows to serve God, and that they were Sisters in a Christian Order that was based on the ancient teachings. She said they did not belong to any denomination, but rather simply sought to follow the teachings and examples of Jesus Christ and Mary, His mother. The class, once again, opened up an entirely new understanding and insight into both the Christian teachings and into myself. I was amazed. And once again, by the time I left I was pondering that light I'd seen in this Sister's eyes, too—and how the spiritual exercises they gave us affected me so intensely. I felt light and stillness inside my being for hours following the class.

I was in a quandary: How could I feel so intensely resistant to receiving teaching from a spiritual form that was Christian, and at the same time feel so attracted to what I experienced at that order house? I liked thinking of myself as an aspiring yogi and rejected the thought of being defined as a Christian. And yet, my intuition told me that there, in that Christian path, I would be able to find the teaching and the spiritual growth and development that I sought. Simultaneously, to my own dismay, I realized that the yogic path I was on was not likely to take me very far. When I looked at the people around me in the ashram and when I looked at myself, I saw that we had changed externally in that we were living a more disciplined life, full of spiritual practices and teachings. But none of us seemed to be changing much in terms of our emotional struggles and psychological issues. We had no one to help us work these challenges out. No one helped us face ourselves and address what our individual barriers were to spiritual growth. I was seeing ever more clearly that spiritual practices and studies without individual and ongoing direction through a teacher who knew me well were not going to change me enough for me to even approach any possibility of entering into a state of being filled with Light. I had read of such experiences, and yet I saw no way that my current practices could lead me into such a state of enlightenment. Somehow, though, these women who taught at the mystical Christian center seemed to be obtaining the kind of transformative help that I knew I was missing. How could this be?

When I spoke with the Sisters at the order house, they told me that they had Sunday services, too, and invited me to experience one. After several weeks, I finally agreed to go. The chapel looked a lot like a Catholic chapel. Candles burned on the altar, upon which a blue flame also glowed. They told me this was called an eternal flame and represented the flame of the God-Self within us. Above the altar was a central cross, and on each side were pictures of Jesus and Mary. These were not pictures I had ever seen before, and they were disturbingly moving. The Jesus in the picture was not sappy sweet nor excruciatingly persecuted, as I had seen Him in other pictures. He felt more like a spiritual master, and I saw both depth of knowing and loving kindness in His eyes. The Mary picture moved me deeply, for I saw Her purity and simplicity, as well as the power that moved through Her.

The service consisted of singing and a sermon, which was followed by the serving of communion. Everyone knelt when being served communion, and each person was given an individual blessing after receiving it. When the Sister laid her hand on my head to bless me, I felt power and light flow into me as I had never experienced it before. My inner struggle between attraction to and repulsion by this path became intense. After the service, the Sisters asked me what I felt. I exclaimed, "If you could just get that picture of Jesus off the altar, I would love this place!" I was surprised to find that my issue with Jesus did not offend them, nor did they consider me a great and hopeless sinner. They told me that they had had similar issues when they first encountered this path, and they understood how hard it could be. I was puzzled by their acceptance of my resistance and of me. I was still full of the feeling receiving communion had left in me: A sense of being filled with a powerful spiritual substance that was now moving through my body and bringing light to its every cell.

After attending a few more classes and services at the order house, I asked them what I would need to do if I wanted to get involved with this path. They told me that baptism was the first step. I said I had been baptized. They explained that their baptism was different. This baptism would be the conscious beginning of my asking Jesus and Mary to teach me and lead me on the inner path to God. Those two illustrious Beings would then take me to my teachers on Earth. I would not be baptized into a church, but rather into Jesus and Mary as the great teachers within me. By this time, I still had *some* resistance to Jesus but had managed to drop enough of it to know it would be a good thing to be taught by Him directly. I realized that my resistance was actually against the institutions that bore His name and that He Himself was most likely a wonderful being with whom I would be quite blessed to have any kind of relationship. With this understanding, I asked for baptism and was scheduled to receive it on Easter morning of 1977.

A woman priest came to the Center to perform the Easter service. She baptized me while she was there. After the service, I had a chance to talk with her for a bit. I asked her about her path and how long she had to train to be a priest in this order. She said she had been trained for seven years before ordination. I was appalled. Seven years? To my 23-year-old mind, that was a very long training period. Little did I know at the time that it would be 19 years of various kinds of training and innumerable successes and failures, joys and sorrows, before I would be ordained a priest! Talking with this priest and seeing her in action did arouse the first inkling of a thought that maybe I would like to do such work. When I asked her how I might go about that, she told me that I would have to begin with a two-year celibate period during which I would be trained and then sent out to do mission work. Trainees in this program could therefore not be married or parenting at the time. They could get married later, but could not be during the time of training. My brief vision of perhaps wanting to obtain priest training in this order was quickly destroyed. Since I had a husband and two children, I was clearly not eligible for such training. Had I once again come across a path that would not take me very far? I felt immensely let down and wondered whether I would ever find a path that would work for me.

Once I recovered from my disappointment enough to reason, it occurred to me that maybe I should try to find a spiritual teacher who could and would really teach me, and agree to do whatever path he or she was doing. Maybe I had gone about this the wrong way: trying to find a path first, only to find out I had no access to real teachers or to advancement on that path. I knew this Christian path I had found clearly moved spiritual energy. I knew it truly taught and empowered people. Maybe if I found a teacher who agreed to teach me, I would be more likely to get the deep and intense training that I sought.

Sal was very interested in the mystical Islamic teachings, Sufism, and especially in particular teachings by a man named G.I. Gurdjieff, an Aramaic teacher who came to have some influence in the late 40s, especially in France and England. His students took his teachings to the USA and many other countries. Sal wanted to go to the Gurdjieff training school in West Virginia for their 10-month basic training course. I was so glad that Sal wanted to do something spiritual that I agreed to go along and also be a student there for the year. I hoped this might lead me a step closer to finding my teacher and my path. Since no other means had worked, I was open to exploring yet another spiritual practice that some said worked for them. I was, in fact, going to gain much through my time in this Sufi-oriented school. But was I to find a true path and teacher there? It was a blessing that I did not know that I was still years away from reaching that goal, or I might have given up. I would give birth to two more children and encounter several more life changes before the day arrived when I met the man who brought me into a state of illumination that changed my being for life.

The Baby I Lost Comes and Gives Answers to My Questions

One night during this period, I was sitting in the kids' room at home nursing Nathan. Odessa was sleeping beside me. The early evening sun was still dimly shining through the open window. I listened to the birds chirping outside. It was a perfectly beautiful, idyllic, mothering moment. I looked down at Nathan—chubby, healthy, blissfully sleeping at my breast. My heart filled with joy at how contented he was. Suddenly, I imagined my first son, Ian, saying, "You never held *me* like that!" I had never before considered how he might feel about how I nurtured my other two kids. Now the imaginary voice toppled me from the seventh heaven of maternal bliss to what felt like the seventh hell. I burst into tears. I cried out: "Ian, Ian, I am so sorry! You should not have had to die alone! I should have been there with you! I am so, so sorry!"

As I sobbed, I heard a voice say, "Mother!" I looked over to Odessa, who was sleeping. I looked at Nathan, who was also sleeping and could not yet speak. Who else could be calling me "Mother"? I raised my eyes and there before me was a vision of a boy, about five years old, brilliantly shining with light. Once again he said, "Mother!" I immediately knew it was Ian. He had the same bright blue eyes and jet-black hair, and he felt the same to me. He appeared at the age he would have been if he had lived. More tears gushed from my eyes as I saw him standing there. I begged his forgiveness for not having been with him when he was sick and when he died. For all I knew he might have died of a broken heart, thinking I had abandoned him. After listening to my teary apologies, he said very simply: "Mother, everything was exactly as it needed to be. You did nothing wrong." He went on to tell me that he needed to live just four days, and he needed to die alone, in a machine. All was exactly right for the needs of his soul. I tried to protest that maybe it was right for him, but I still failed as a mother. Ian once again assured me I had done nothing wrong. As he was there before me, obviously thriving, I had to accept that he must know. To this day, I am so grateful for his appearance to me and for his assurance of the rightness of his death and its circumstances.

Oftentimes when I lecture or when I am counseling students, I am asked how God could be a loving God and yet allow terrible things to happen to people. Often I tell them about Ian. Most people would agree that a baby dying shortly after birth due to inadequate care is a terrible thing. Many would use this as an example of how God is mean, or maybe weak and ineffective, or else such things would not be allowed to happen. Yet, Ian told me himself that what happened was exactly how he needed it to be. That Ian was gone was certainly extremely painful to those of us who had looked forward to spending our lives with him. Many tears were shed over his death. But was it a terrible thing? Is an event that hurts us deeply and grieves us for a long time necessarily a terrible thing?

Most of the time, we have a quite limited vision upon which we base our judgments of what is good and what is bad. If something makes us feel good, we generally assume it is good. If it hurts, we think it must be bad. This reasoning is hardly beyond the level of a five-year old, and yet it dominates most people's thinking and judgment of the world and the justice of God. We are, however, not creatures of one lifetime and one dimension only, namely that of physical existence. We are instead creatures of many lifetimes, souls that need certain experiences to continue our development. This truth became so clear to me through Ian's life, death, and reappearance. As discussed before, we often need some difficult and painful experiences in order to swiftly and clearly learn the lessons we need. We incarnate with a family that also needs certain experiences to grow. With our input and consent and the help of beings of light, our needs are matched with our families' needs before we incarnate.

Ian needed only four days. I needed to learn about losing a baby, which later allowed me to help many of my midwifery and counseling clients deal with infant losses. I also learned the lesson stated here pertaining to the rightness of things that happen to us. This story alone has helped many a person change their perspective from being angry with God to opening up to a greater vision of life and reality. Sal received another set of lessons from the experience. We were all greatly blessed. What a perfect match of lessons that needed to be learned! I am still awed at the greatness of how the plans are laid out for each human being so that we can receive everything we need to progress toward wholeness and unity with the Self within. Is God ever mean? God is only mean to the extent that you cannot see beyond the smallest of pictures. Is God ever stupid? Only as far as your understanding is limited regarding what purpose we all have for being on earth.

5

A GUIDE FOR MY SOUL: FINDING A TRUE SPIRITUAL TEACHER

Oh heart, sit with someone who knows the heart;
Go under the tree, which has fresh blossoms.

—Rumi, *The Mathnawi*, 1926 (English Translation)

Life at the Sufi School

In August of 1977, Sal and I took our two children and moved to Charles Town, West Virginia, to begin a 10-month study of Sufism and the teachings of G.I. Gurdjieff. I had no idea what to expect from this school, as I had not read any of Gurdjieff's writings. However, since my efforts to find a teacher and a path were not bearing much fruit, and Sal wanted to attend this school, I agreed. Maybe this would be another step along the way to finding my way to God. Sal, the kids, and I moved into one room, which we roughly divided in half through the use of shelves to make somewhat separate spaces for the children and for us. We ate all our meals with the other students and the staff members. Our children had never been in childcare for more than short periods. I had some concerns about how they would take to this new situation. To my relief, they soon became accustomed to spending most of each day with the childcare providers, along with the other eight children whose parents were our fellow students.

Each day began at six a.m. with meditation and "Morning Exercise." This term was used for spiritual exercises Gurdjieff gave his students. These exercises were intended to help us become conscious of the spiritual forces within our own being and in the universe. Once conscious of those forces, we can begin to work with them to effect change. After Morning Exercise, breakfast was served, usually followed by a class. One of the classes taught was a form of sacred dance, or what in Gurdjieff circles is called "Movements." Gurdjieff was said to have gathered these dances and Movements from various Eastern and Middle Eastern cultures, and some were ostensibly in their original form from ancient Egyptian culture. We also received instruction in color meditation and healing, taught by an Indian Buddhist monk who was in his 80s. We had courses in art and the unconscious mind, taught by a Jungian analyst. And each day the headmaster read to us from Gurdjieff's writings.

After lunch, we generally had "Practical Work," during which we were assigned various jobs around the school's extensive grounds. During these external work times, we were given inner spiritual work to do. Usually they gave us a reminder every half hour for us to stop working, focus on the thought or inner exercise assigned for that day, and become aware of where we had drifted to in mind and emotion. We worked in all weather conditions, including pouring rain, snow, and sleet. The inclement weather tended to bring out various negative emotions in us students, which our teachers informed us were all the more useful for us to examine so we could see and understand ourselves better. I found these to be quite fruitful indeed. When working in soaking clothes on jobs that seemed useless, I saw how negative I could get and how much I tried to find excuses to get out of the work.

Some assignments were intentionally set up to arouse our most negative reactions. One time a group of us were told to dig a long ditch about three feet deep. The weather was cold and rainy. As we worked, the headmaster came around several times, telling us to work harder, dig deeper, do better. It seemed to be a most important job, judging by the attention the headmaster was giving it. We were not to ask why on such jobs, and instead our instructors recommended that we simply try to be obedient to the orders they gave us. After hours of freezing and backbreaking work, the headmaster came by, inspected the completed ditch, and then summarily told us to fill it back in. I immediately recognized that this must be a spiritual exercise and smiled to myself. However, some of my classmates could not accept this as a learning opportunity and disintegrated in a torrent of accusations and self-pity. The headmaster watched us fill the ditch back in with the same sense of grave importance that he had held about digging it in the first place. When we returned to our residence hall sore, soaked and exhausted, a rare treat of hot chocolate and fresh baked pastries awaited us. As I ate them, I pondered what had occurred outside and inside of me during that day, and felt grateful for the teaching they had given me. The day's events made my resistance to hard work, and especially hard work while I was getting wet and cold, quite obvious. I had to acknowledge that I tended to cater to my physical comfort and often even used my duties as a mother as an excuse to get out of such uncomfortable physical work. Yes, I was able to switch over more quickly than some to recognizing the worth of the exercise as a spiritual one, yet my inner grumbling about having to do such work had surely been as present as anyone else's.

Food was another arena that the teachers used to bring the students into an awareness of their attachments, concepts, and rigidity. Some days we were simply not given enough food. The portions would be small, with no seconds. Other days we were given only very meager arrays of food, such as meals made up of boiled turnips. These practices were not very distressing to me, since I'd already had years of practice from my yogic life of fasting and depriving myself of various food luxuries, but some of the other students fell apart. These food experiences brought out aspects of some of the students' characters that had previously not been apparent. I felt surprised and somewhat shocked by seeing the intensity of people's ideas about their food, and what a hindrance those attachments can be to inner growth. I was glad I had already overcome a number of fears and struggles related to food.

The headmaster looked for other ways to help us come face to face with our pride, ambitions, concepts, and attitudes. One of the students was a very hard-to-tolerate fellow who had a knack for upsetting and aggravating almost everyone who had any dealings with him. People dreaded having to work with him. Gurdjieff was said to have intentionally recruited especially obnoxious characters into his programs because they were such catalysts for bringing out everyone else's worst sides. Many of us suspected that this particular student had been brought into the course for such a reason. To sit beside the headmaster during meals and get to speak with him while eating was considered a great privilege. Each of us would hope to have that honor but would worry about getting nailed for being ambitious or greedy if we took a seat beside him. At each meal there was some to-do in each of our minds and emotions about where to sit. Personally, I kept a close eye on who was sitting with the headmaster, and how that person's interaction with him was going. I was distressed to notice that I had a keen desire to sit by the teacher and make a favorable impression on him. I coveted his attention and recognition. And yet I was afraid of his reprimands and the embarrassment I would feel if he called me on my prideful attitude. I did sit there once or twice, but mostly stayed away while observing how others who sat near this teacher fared.

Our headmaster began to make a practice of inviting this particularly difficult student to sit next to him. The student was obviously not only flattered but quite proud, taking this invitation to mean that he was indeed above the rest of us. He spent these meals arrogantly telling the headmaster of his various exploits and accomplishments. Many of us had experienced the pain of the headmaster's piercing look or the sting of his words when he pointed out to us how prideful we were, or the unconsciousness of our speaking. With this student, however, the headmaster listened attentively and seemed deeply interested and impressed with what the student was saying. The headmaster's favorable attitude toward this student did not go unnoticed by many of the other students. The headmaster's behavior had what I presumed was his desired effect: Many a student, including myself at times, became angry with him. How could he prefer this pompous, difficult person above us? Couldn't he see that he was making the student even more arrogant and insufferable? Why was he nice to him and not to us? Much of my own baggage became apparent to me through this seemingly small practice that our headmaster embraced. I felt the sting of having to acknowledge how much I wanted approval from this teacher, and how selfish and uncompassionate I was toward this student, who obviously had many issues. That particular student, to the headmaster's apparently great dismay and many other students' great relief, had a psychological breakdown a couple of months into our course and had to leave the program to receive treatment.

Our instructors wanted to expose us to "real" Sufis, meaning people who were actually working as teachers and students from the Near-and Middle East. One weekend we traveled by bus to New York State to visit with a Sheikh Mussafer from a Sufi order called the "Helvetis." The Sheikh received us and, as he was Turkish, spoke with us through an interpreter. His authority moved us. He invited us to an event in which he was leading his dervishes (students) into a mystical ecstatic trance through song and dance. Once the dervishes were deeply into this mystical state, some of them drove large pins and needles straight through their cheeks, lips, or noses, without showing any signs of pain. It was a different kind of practice than I had ever seen, and I tried to hold it within me and be grateful that this Sheikh and his dervishes were willing to invite us into their sacred ritual. I could not imagine engaging in the practices they maintained, and I did not understand how their body piercing drew them close to God. I did, however, sense that they were, in fact, drawn into a spiritual experience through their practices, and I felt a deep respect for them for being so dedicated.

Before I came to the Sufi school, the Sisters from the Christian Order gave me a book that contained the basic lessons and some spiritual exercises I was to do; one for each month. They also gave me the name of a priest to whom I was to send my notes regarding my experiences with the exercises. I had begun to feel a connection with Jesus and Mary, and did not want to lose that while away at this school. I faithfully did my exercises from the order alongside the Gurdjieff and Sufi work I was being given. I told the headmaster that I was doing this and obtained his consent. I was sure of the reality of what I had experienced with the Order and I knew I had committed to Jesus and Mary, to allow Them to teach me. I therefore did not want to drop my end of the agreement, and was glad the headmaster honored my commitment.

While still in Louisville, I had also begun to feel great blessings and benefits from receiving communion at the order house. I was often stunned at the profundity of the experience. The powerful influx of energy and presence far surpassed my mind's ability to comprehend or explain. I had only started to know that receiving communion was changing me from the inside out, without my conscious mind having any idea of how this was happening. Because of the blessings I had experienced from receiving communion regularly, I now, though in West Virginia, still longed to receive it. I looked around to see what possibilities for communion might be in the area. I found a Roman Catholic Trappist monastery that was only a 15-minute drive away. One of my fellow students was a devout Roman Catholic, so she and I began attending Sunday services at the monastery. My friend taught me what I needed to know to receive communion in this setting. I knew that the Catholics might disapprove of my receiving it as a non-Catholic. But I also felt powerfully within my heart that Jesus would not turn me away, and the respect and devotion with which I received it was what mattered. My initial partaking of communion was clumsy enough that I felt sure the monks were aware that I was not Catholic. In addition, I did not know when to kneel and when to rise, and at first I knew none of the responses and prayers expected of the congregation. Only 6 to 12 people came to mass there on Sundays, along with the monks, so my lack of knowledge of the mass was most likely noticed. But my heart became so full of joy at each mass that it seemed to me that the monks saw that joy and were glad to have me join them, Catholic or not.

When other students heard me say how much mass had come to mean to me, a number of them asked to come along. Over the weeks, more and more joined me until my large International station wagon was often filled to the brim with about a dozen students going to mass with the monks. Almost none of them were Catholic, so I taught them how to receive communion on the way to the monastery. The monks were quite amazed at the doubling of the number of people attending Sunday mass. Obviously these people I brought were not Catholic, but the students were often so moved by the mass that they wept as they received communion. I think the monks had not seen so much feeling and appreciation regarding communion in many years, and they welcomed us heartily each Sunday. The Abbott figured out that I must be the ringleader, and one Sunday he invited me in to speak with him. He was most interested in hearing about the spiritual training we were involved in and said that some day he would like to meet our headmaster and see our school.

In the Christian tradition, the four weeks before Christmas are called the Season of Advent. I was most excited to delve into Advent, as this was to be the first year I would be entering it with some consciousness as to its deeper import and meaning. The Order sent me a special practice to prepare for Christmas, and I was eagerly attending Sunday masses at the monastery. The day before Christmas Eve, when I was high with anticipation of attending Christmas mass, the headmaster informed the students that he was not happy with some of us leaving each Sunday to go to the monastery. He said he suspected we were looking to get out of Practical Work, and we were cheating our fellow students. He therefore forbade us to attend mass anymore. He told us that he was very serious about this and that any student who went to mass might quite possibly be expelled from the program.

After carefully searching my heart and conscience, I decided to go anyhow. The woman who was Roman Catholic and had been coming with me from the beginning decided—independently of me—to do the same. The others were all horrified that we were choosing to go against the orders. They were afraid of being expelled. My friend and I, however, felt we had a higher commitment than to this school, and we were not to miss the celebration of Jesus' birth, for which we had been preparing for weeks. As we walked out of the building that morning, a number of students followed us with their eyes. Some even launched a last-ditch effort to talk us out of this move while we were going through the door. They had grown fond of us and would have hated to see us expelled. We did not know what would happen to us upon our return, but we felt certain we had to go.

I was so excited to be celebrating the Master Jesus' birth for the first time with growing consciousness of its meaning that I was able to clear my mind of any worry of what was in store for us upon our return to the school. I now felt a bit of what that birth meant inside my being. I had been hearing from the order that all the events and characters in the New Testament symbolize something inside us, so I had been preparing to experience, for the first time, the meaning of that birth. I was not disappointed. I had a great experience of the light, how it comes to be within us, and how it is born into greater reality with the celebration of Christ's birth. In a highly elevated state of awe and gratitude, I returned to the school.

The headmaster awaited us at the door. A number of students stood around wanting to see what would happen. The other woman and I approached the door. My heart was pounding. I wondered what would befall us. What if I was expelled? What would Sal do? Would he stay though I'd left? How about the kids? These considerations occupied my heart and mind as we approached the sullen-faced teacher. He asked us where we had been. We told him we had gone to mass. He asked whether we had heard him forbidding anyone to go. We said we had. He spoke to us in a very grave manner. Then his face softened, he smiled, and said, "Well done! You two were right to go. The others were right not to." We were astonished, thrilled, and relieved. The headmaster invited us to sit with him for lunch and he told us some stories to illustrate the importance of knowing one's own conscience, and when to follow orders and when to not follow them. I felt doubly blessed on that Christmas day.

Why Do We Need a Spiritual Teacher?

The well-known mystical Jewish theologian, Martin Buber, wrote:

> We do, indeed, know that all that is necessary is to have a soul united within itself and indivisibly directed to its divine goal. But how, in the chaos of life on our earth, are we to keep the holy goal in sight? How retain the unity in the midst of peril and pressure, in the midst of thousands of disappointments and delusions? And once unity is lost, how recover it? Man needs counsel and aid; he must be lifted and redeemed. And he does not need all this only in regard to his soul, for in some way or other, the domains of the soul are intertwined with the big and little cares, the griefs and despairs of life itself, and if these are not dealt with, how shall those loftiest concerns be approached? A helper is needed, a helper for both body and soul, for both earthly and heavenly matters. This helper is called the Zaddik (the spiritual master). He can heal both the ailing body and the ailing soul, for he knows how one is bound up with the other, and this knowledge gives him the power to influence both. It is he who can teach you to conduct your affairs so that your soul remains free, and he can teach you to strengthen your soul, to keep you steadfast beneath the blows of destiny. And over and over he takes you by the hand and guides you until you can walk alone. (Martin Buber, *Tales of the Hasidism*, 1948.)

A popular Sufi saying is: "Whoever travels without a guide needs two hundred years for a day's journey." Another is: "One might read all the books of instruction for a thousand years, but without a guide nothing would be achieved." So both mystical Jewish and mystical Islamic sources taught the necessity and the great blessedness of having a teacher. I knew in my heart that these sayings were true. I also had met enough spiritual teachers in various kinds of schools to develop some knowledge of what a real teacher is. Basically, unless a person has not only entered into the God-Self within their being but has also been taught and empowered to bring other people into that initiation, they will not be able to take a student as far as he or she might otherwise be able to go. Many teachers can open a student's eyes to great truths and inspirations, but few Teachers have all the keys to the inner realms and are accessible to teach students who seek them out.

One can choose to work with all kinds of teachers, but if one is serious about having the option to go through all the initiations into the realm of Self, then one will need a real master teacher. Do not let yourself be deceived by fancy titles. Anyone can carry such a title. But now that you have a description of what the Path actually is, you will be able to ask questions of any purported teachers to find out what they have to offer. Never agree to go against your ethics. Sex and excesses of money should never be part of the agreement to be taught. No real teacher who is in accord with God would have intercourse with a student. No real teacher would seek to become wealthy in exchange for teaching the great Truths of all ages. Do not be deceived, but don't give up if what you really want is to be taught. Pray to find a school and a teacher. Make yourself ready to be a student, and your prayers will be answered.

The Whirling Dervish, The Teacher Who Was Not a Teacher, and The Joy of Finding The Teacher Who Could and Would Teach Me

Toward the end of our year at the Gurdjieff school, we had the great honor of having the head of the Mevlevi Sufi Order come to see us from Turkey. The Mevlevis are the Whirling Dervishes. Though some other orders whirl, the Mevlevis are best known for this sacred dance practice. Their sheikh was in his 80s and was only about four feet, eight inches tall. I was very happy that I was going to get to meet this man that I had heard so much about. His name was Suleyman Dede. He was one of our headmaster's spiritual teachers and had initiated our headmaster into various Sufi practices. As we all gathered on the floor of our assembly hall, sitting on pillows, waiting for Dede's arrival, an air of expectancy permeated our hearts and minds.

Dede arrived with his entourage of about eight dervishes. Dervishes are students of a Sufi teacher. They sometimes all live together in one place, or they may also live nearby where they can spend much of their time at the center with the teacher. When Dede came in, we rose in respect. After we sat back down, this little man stood before us, and looking all around at us he began to weep. Big tears ran down his cheeks as we all sat in astonishment, not knowing what was going on. Dede spoke Turkish and over and over brought his hands together as in prayer. He looked up toward the sky and back down at us, weeping. Finally, someone who spoke English and Turkish stood up and translated what Dede was saying. He said that Dede was overwhelmed with gratitude that God was allowing him to meet all of us. As he wept, he explained that it was such an honor to be there with us that his heart was overflowing with joy and love for us. There stood this little old holy man, weeping and praising God for the great honor of getting to meet this motley crew of regular Americans who were just beginning to learn about Sufism and spiritual life.

I had been watching, feeling quite distressed as he wept, even before the translator told us what Dede was saying. I felt pain in my chest, as my heart was torn open in the face of such beautiful humility. This man, this great teacher, was *that* grateful to meet *us*! Us, the nothings of this world! It was *we* who should have been feeling that way about meeting *him*! The contrast between our own lack of humility and his great humility was too painful to bear in my heart. I, too, began to weep. I do not remember anything else that Dede said through the translator. I only know I continued to weep for several hours, even after everyone else had left the hall. What a blessing to be taught such a deep and powerful lesson simply by the demonstration of true humility. We did not even need a language in common for that lesson to take root in my being. It has never left me, and I am eternally grateful to Sheikh Suleyman Dede for giving me that gift.

Later that day, the abbot from the Trappist monastery joined Dede and our headmaster for a feast prepared by Dede himself. Though Dede was so gentle and kind with us, the students he was visiting, we saw what strict discipline he expected from his own students. His orders were crisp and followed without a word or a moment's delay. He told his dervishes what each was to do for the preparation of the meal. Dede still regarded our own headmaster, who must have been nearly 60 years old, as his student. When getting ready to prepare the meal, Dede told our headmaster to sit on the chair he placed in the middle of the kitchen, then told him that his job was to pray. Dede said it with such intensity that we all got the message that this was not just chatting with God, but something very serious. So our teacher prayed silently, for all of the three to four hours of the preparation of the meal. What happened in that kitchen was not ordinary meal preparation. Sacred nourishment was being prepared, and the atmosphere was one of a ritual.

The abbot greatly enjoyed talking with our headmaster and with Dede. Most of the time a translator was there to help. But once I glanced over and noticed that the translator must have stepped out for a moment. The Abbot and Dede were talking with each other, one in English and one in Turkish, and the spirit of their exchange far surpassed the language barrier, for they were both clearly communicating and enjoying each other's company. What a beautiful joining of spirits: The Trappist abbot, the Turkish Sufi sheikh, and the English-born headmaster, all sharing the joys and tribulations of trying to bring students into relationship with God. They even spoke of possibly exchanging students for a while to teach them different things.

Throughout the year I had many spiritual experiences. These experiences came during meditation, during Movements classes, or during Practical Work. And sometimes they came when I was not doing anything in particular. Most days we had a time for gathering and sharing what was going on with each of us. I often felt badly that I almost always had something wonderful and amazing to tell. Most other people only had occasional experiences to report. Visions and perceptions were opening to my spiritual senses that I had never known were there to be perceived, and we were told to share whatever we were experiencing. I became aware that I was drawing the ire of some of my fellow students. I did not know what to do about their reactions. One day a woman came up to me and told me that she was furious with me. She said that she thought it was so unfair that I would have all these experiences because I had only come along to be with my husband. Everyone else had prepared for years, studying the writings of Gurdjieff, taking part in local groups, doing some work on their own, yet most of their spiritual experiences seemed to be few and far between. Why was it different for me? she asked.

I told her that the only explanation I had was that I was baptized just before coming there. She was incredulous. "What could that have to do with it?" she demanded. I told her that in baptism I had asked that Jesus and Mary take me on as a Their student and begin to teach me the Inner Path. It seemed to me now that they had taken me seriously and were using whatever means were available to begin to develop me spiritually under Their tutelage. Until now, I had not deeply examined what was, in fact, happening to me, or why. I myself was awed by the concept that these great Beings might in fact be teaching me. The woman went away perplexed.

The year came to an end. In the last weeks, we were all brought in groups of three or four at a time to the headmaster's house and were initiated into a *zikr*. A zikr is a practice somewhat like meditating with a mantra, somewhat like a Christian repetitive prayer, that can only be handed down from people whose teachers authorized them to do so to students of their own. Our headmaster had been given this right by his teacher and now initiated us all into it. It was a very solemn thing to have one's name called and to walk to our headmaster's cottage and be taught how to pray this zikr. It felt like a great honor and part of a very old tradition.

In the last week, we were each granted a meeting with the headmaster if we so desired. I had come to appreciate how much I had learned here, and I had great hopes that maybe the headmaster would take me on as his student, and I would thereby have found a spiritual teacher. When I went into his room, I told him that I wanted to go as far as I could in this life, and would he please take me on as his student. The headmaster was facing the window as I spoke. When he turned around, he had tears coming down his cheeks. I was startled and asked if I had said something to offend him. He said, "I am so sorry, but I cannot teach you. You need a real teacher, and that is not what I am."

I was so astonished I hardly knew what to say. "But what do you mean you are not a real teacher? You are the headmaster of a Gurdjieff/Sufi training program and school. How can you not be a teacher?" I exclaimed.

He said, "All I do is try to begin to wake people up. I know you are sincere. I have been watching you. I know what a real teacher is because I had real teachers myself. But that is not what I am." My heart sank. Had I reached another dead end on my quest for a spiritual teacher?

"So where do you suggest that I find such a real teacher?" I asked him.

"It is my sense that yours is the Christian path. You will need to find a Christian teacher," he said.

"And where shall I go to find a Christian teacher?" I asked.

"I don't know," he said. "I have never met one."

I walked out of that cottage feeling more lost than ever. I also felt deep respect for the headmaster for being so humble and honest. That certainly was more than I had experienced with the several yogis I had asked to teach me. But what was I to do now? The only place I knew that had Christian teachers was the Order where I was baptized, and they would not accept anyone who was married and parenting into higher-level training. I felt directionless and wondered whether I would ever find a teacher. My desire for nothing more was clear and definite. Surely there had to be a way somehow, somewhere.

I left the school in June of 1978 and moved back to Kentucky. My marriage had taken quite a beating during the time at school. Most of the relationships there did. People were going through big changes, and there was no counseling or help available for couples needing it. Living in community and taking all meals in common with everyone also allowed for very little couple time. All these factors contributed to a dismally high rate of separation and divorce among course participants and graduates. The temptation to be unfaithful was also very high due to living so closely with many people. Since the course offered no particular ethical guidelines in these matters, everyone was free to do whatever they chose. During those months my marriage suffered mostly from neglect. It took Sal and me much of the next year to recover from the damage. This seemed wrong to me, that a spiritual school would not offer help to couples and would not be more aware of what couples needed to survive such a year. I made a note to myself that if I ever had anything to do with how a spiritual school was run, I would make sure that the same errors were not made in these matters.

When we got back to Kentucky, I began a midwifery practice. I attended home births and did some labor support for hospital births. The first woman whose birth I attended became my midwifery partner and a good friend. Her name was Nancy. Sal and I decided to join with Nancy and her husband and buy 130 acres in rural Kentucky for the purpose of developing our homesteads. We split the land roughly down the middle and built houses and barns, each on our own side. For the first two years, we did not have running water, and another year passed before we had running hot water. We moved out to the land in 1980. We now had a third child, Pascale, who was born in 1979. For six months, we lived in a school bus that was outfitted to be a camper while Sal built us a fairly primitive passive solar house. We moved in as soon as it had windows and a roof, but long before it was finished. I gave birth there in 1981 to our fourth child, Sofia. It was a hard life, though it also filled us with the joys of living off the land and raising our children in a natural paradise. Nancy and I had a busy midwifery practice. We introduced a midwifery bill into the legislature and lobbied it ourselves. It passed in the Senate and died in the House. We sued the Health Department for not licensing us. When that failed, we helped a man who promised support for our cause run for governor. When his bid for governor failed, we declared ourselves truly burnt out with politics, having at that point tried to bring about change for midwifery in Kentucky through the legislative, judicial, and executive branches—and not succeeding. It was, however, quite an adventure and an education. I felt I received a lasting lesson from all this political work: I now knew that regular little people such as I could take on tasks that seem virtually undoable and sometimes succeed at them. This lesson was to prove extremely important years later, when I was faced with starting a spiritual order. I kept a button on my desk that read, "You cannot achieve the impossible if you do not attempt the absurd."

Living on our little farm, we grew almost all our own food and home-schooled the kids. I tried to keep a meditation and prayer practice going. I had completed a correspondence course with the Order that baptized me and now had no idea what else I could do. Not a day went by when I did not long to be learning from a teacher and going as far as I could spiritually in this life. Then, in the summer of 1983, I got a call from the same friend who had told me about the Order when I was living in the yoga ashram. He told me that there was a newly formed off-shoot of the previous order that offered the same training as the former one but also offered it to married and parenting people. He told me there were two master teachers about three hours' drive from where I was living, and that he thought they would be willing to meet with me.

I was afraid to get my hopes up too much. I called the teachers that my friend had told me about. They seemed approachable and asked me to come see them. My appointment to meet them came after I had been up all night with an extremely difficult birth, but I was determined to keep that appointment. When I got to their house, I found them to be warm and welcoming. Then came the moment to ask the question I had been asking teachers all over the country for the past 10 years. I said to Master Peter, "Spiritually, I want to go as far as I can in this life. I don't know where I am on the Path. I only know that I want to keep moving ahead in my growth. I will do anything within ethical limits that I need to do to be taught. Will you teach me?"

Master Peter answered, "This is where you are on the Path [and he explained it]. This is where there is to go [and he explained it based on initiations and ordinations available within this order]. When do you want to start?" I gathered from what Master Peter said that he could see that I had developed some light in my being through the years of spiritual practices and exercises. I would, however, need some individual instruction in the areas of my life, my thinking, and my feelings that were still laced with negative patterns. He told me that he could see me coming into the initiation of illumination, and even Self-realization in time, if I allowed myself to be taught. If later on I felt called to serve as a minister, that training could also be an option.

My heart nearly burst with joy. I could not believe it! Finally, I had found a true Path and a teacher who would teach me, without any limits being set on my potential advancement, as long as I did the work and submitted to the training and transformation. All the way home, I could not get the smile off my face. I had no trouble staying awake at the wheel, even though I had been up all of the previous night. Master Peter had explained what a real spiritual Path is and how one moves along it through the initiations. It was hard to grasp what these initiations would be like, and how I could possibly become spiritual enough to deserve them. I understood they had something to do with divine light filling me and changing me, and that nothing would be the same again. But how was this to happen? I had no idea. However, my intuition told me that I had finally found my way to the means by which I could grow, be transformed, and hopefully serve God. For now, I had to try to relax into the process without the benefit of knowing what it would be like. I knew I had to trust, and I decided I would.

My training began that day. Master Peter gave me studies and spiritual exercises to do. I was to have a long meeting on the phone with him each week, and attend classes and Sunday services at his house whenever I could. I knew I was finally home, in the school that would train me, and that I would never need to search again. I was now 29 years old, and had been seeking my spiritual Path for 10 years.

6

BECOMING AS CLAY IN THE HANDS OF THE MASTER: LEARNING TO BE A SPIRITUAL STUDENT

"The Master watches every moment of the disciple's spiritual growth; he watches him particularly during his forty-day period of meditation that became, very early, a regular institution in the Sufi path... The sheikh interprets the murid's (disciple's) dreams and visions, reads his thoughts, and thus follows every movement of his conscious and subconscious life... In the hands of the master the murid should be as passive as a corpse in the hands of the undertaker."

—Annemarie Schimmel, *Mystical Dimensions of Islam*

Initial Experiences and Surprises as a New Student Working With a Teacher

Finally, I had found the spiritual teacher I had been looking for all my adult life. I imagined that I would soon become quite holy and enter into various kinds of exalted states, and my feet would hardly touch the earth anymore. My disposition would become so peaceful and balanced that my family would have to honor my new state of being and would be so moved by it that they would become full of holy peace themselves. Like most new students working with a spiritual teacher, I had not understood what the Path to achieving that balance would entail. I was somewhat stunned when my teacher not only acknowledged my spiritual experiences and states but also addressed my shortcomings and not-so-spiritual concepts, attitudes, habits, and behaviors. I felt embarrassed that my foibles and assorted negativities were up for review, and also worried that once he really saw me for what I was, he might not want to teach me anymore.

As I had completed the first and second level of courses through the previous order, mostly by correspondence, Master Peter began my training from that point forward. He gave me readings and spiritual exercises that were much more intense than anything I had previously studied or experienced. At the time, I didn't realize that the intensity also had to do with the fact that now there was the power of the teacher involved in my training, and that this raised the experience to a whole new level. I was for the first time finding out why, as the Sufis say, the growth that takes a day with a teacher would take 200 years without one. I came to realize that now I was *actually* working with a teacher, as opposed to what I thought was working with a teacher in the yoga ashrams or the Gurdjieff school. Just as the Sufi text told it, Master Peter was in fact reading my thoughts, interpreting my dreams and visions, and watching every movement of my conscious and unconscious mind. He was molding my thoughts and feelings into a more wholesome way of being.

It is probably apparent from my life story preceding this time that I was a very independent child and young adult, fiercely determined to do things my own way. Neither my parents nor my husband, Sal, were strangers to my insistence on independence. Allowing myself to be directed and guided was therefore a very new experience for me. Until this point, I tended to launch a quite formidable defense, at least internally, against anyone who had the audacity to criticize me. Now I had to learn to accept correction without defending myself. At first I thought that I was not allowed to say anything at all when a correction was given. It took me some time to realize that if I did not understand what was being referred to or if I did not feel that my teacher's observation fit, I needed to speak up. Master Peter explained to me that by speaking up I offered him a chance to explain himself better so that I could see what he meant, or he could hear me explain myself better so he could understand my situation or position, and could apologize if he had misread or misjudged me. It was a huge relief to learn how to negotiate the waters of being corrected and instructed. It was then that I began to feel love for this teacher, who was wise enough to see the errors in my thinking, feeling, and actions; who cared enough about me and God to put immense time and energy into helping reshape me; and who was humble enough to apologize when he was wrong.

Since I lived more than three hours away from my teacher, I was not able to attend classes and services often. All the other students lived near him. Those stu-

dents attended two classes a week and Sunday services, which included communion. In addition, they had one hour a week of individual instruction and
counseling with him. I longed so much to be able to attend all the classes and Services, but in fact could only do so about once a month. When I *was* able to go, I
took in a Service, a class, and a meeting with him face-to-face, all in one day. The
other students looked somewhat surprised at the enthusiasm I brought to each
visit. They could not understand how hungry I was to learn everything my
teacher offered me, and how much I also longed to be a part of that spiritual
community. I never felt I was there long enough to truly get to know my brothers
and sisters on this Path. I didn't know why it all needed to be so far from me,
after I had waited all those years to find a teacher and a community.

During one of my first visits with Master Peter, he told me to close my eyes
and go deep inside myself. As I did so, I thought I felt him come up beside me
and kneel on the floor and place his hands over my heart, with one hand on my
chest and one on my back, without actually touching me. I went right into an
altered state of consciousness. A big rush of energy welled up from my solar
plexus area in such a powerful motion that it startled me and I jumped a bit. I
opened my eyes to see Master Peter sitting on his chair across the room. I had not
been aware that he had left my side. I asked him when he had sat back down. He
told me he had not left his chair. I was dumbfounded. I recounted to him my
sure sense of his kneeling beside me and placing his hands over my heart, which
then seemed to bring about the immense upwelling of powerful energy within
me. He said that it was not he and that I must have had a visitation by one of the
higher beings who came to give me my first taste of the power of God dwelling
within me. I was stunned and knocked clear out of my reasoning mind. I felt
moved and curious, and yet somehow still inside, all at once. I simply had to
accept that I had had a spiritual experience that I was not going to be able to
explain.

Three Requirements for Working With a Teacher

Learning to be a spiritual student is everyone's first task when beginning to work
with a teacher. Students will face different challenges in attempting to fulfill this
task, depending on their personalities and on their previous experiences with
authority figures. I came to find out later that my own resistance to authority figures stemmed from having had some negative experiences in previous lives.
Because my parents from previous lives had several times tried to keep me from
my choice of a spiritual path or practice, I came into this life full of readiness to

resist anyone trying to control me. Many people are so unwilling to submit to the authority of a spiritual teacher that they would rather not enter upon a Path at all than have to do that. I, however, knew that without a teacher I would not be able to enter the ultimate depth of the mystical training. I therefore consciously chose to override my natural repugnance to submitting to anyone, and in this case, decided to let this teacher teach me. This brings up the whole concept of "submission to a teacher." Does that concept rub you the wrong way? Do you immediately say to yourself, "Why does it have to be submission? Why can't we just talk about studying with a teacher, learning from a teacher, working with a teacher?"

Many people feel they have not fared well when they were under the power of authority figures. Most commonly, these authority figures were the parents or the parent substitutes, but often people have bad experiences with siblings, teachers, employers, and people in the helping professions, such as counselors, doctors, and even ministers. A very important part of healing for those who have been victimized by people who held authority over them is to come to know that they will not have to allow themselves to be victimized again. Now, as a strong adult, they can refuse to allow another person to have power over them. Those who have been victims of physical, sexual, or emotional abuse, need to feel that they have the strength and the power to make their own choices.

For other people, the resistance to submitting to a teacher may not be an issue of being afraid of abuse, but rather a simple issue of pride. To such a person, it would seem unreasonable that any other person should know so much more than they do or be so much more developed spiritually than they are. They would therefore see no need to submit themselves to another person as a student. They would tend to want to go to classes and read books while making sure that they do not get in a position of having to give over the control of their learning or growth. Such people feel proud of being independent and self-formed, and a great hesitancy attached to giving up that freedom. I certainly had my fair share of pride and desire for independence. But I wanted to grow more than I wanted to preserve my pride, and I knew maintaining independence would keep me from what I wanted most. So I swallowed my pride and gratefully accepted my teacher's direction.

For many of us, the word "submission" itself carries connotations of weakness, or perceiving ourselves as less than another. We get images of a dog with its head hanging and its tail between its legs. We feel such images are repulsive when applied to human beings. We are happy to be among the proud and the free, so we see no reason to give up that freedom and turn over that pride. We may feel as if we would be virtually asking for someone to abuse us. We fear losing our delicate sense of self-esteem, for which some of us had to work many years. What about those who still have not healed from the abuse they experienced at the hands of their parents or other caregivers, and who still have not recovered their self-esteem? How are they supposed to come to trust so deeply, and what could they stand to gain from such trust?

The word "submit" comes from the Latin and means "to place under." When we submit to someone or something, we place ourselves under that person or thing. If we submit to a medical procedure, it is because we have decided that we need that procedure and therefore give our permission for the healthcare professionals to perform it. We will not know all the different things that will be done with that procedure. If you have agreed to a triple bypass operation on your heart, you may know basically what will be done. But unless you are a heart surgeon, you will not know what all the steps will be or what tools and medications will be used. You will usually not even know who will be in the operating room with you other than your doctor. Which nurses, scrub technicians, and anesthesiologists will be working on you? Will there be medical students, interns, and residents present? You will have submitted to your doctor overseeing the whole operation and making the decisions necessary as they come up. In your decision, you will have acknowledged that he or she has expertise that you do not have and that you trust him or her to decide what you need and how to go about giving it to you. You will not even be conscious when they will be making life and death decisions regarding you. You do this because you know you need help and you cannot do it for yourself. You may have looked around for surgeons and decided this was the best one. Actually, you have never seen this surgeon operate, so you had to go by what you heard about this doctor and your gut feeling or intuition.

This situation is very similar to the decision to submit to a spiritual teacher. Your so choosing is based on the recognition that you need someone to guide you in doing what you cannot do for yourself. You also recognize that you have no expertise in that particular field of knowledge, so you will not be able to thoroughly evaluate the teacher whom you choose. You can ask around and talk with other students who are studying with that teacher, but you will end up needing to rely on your gut feelings and intuition. Does what this teacher say ring true to you? We all have a sensor within us for what is true. A good time to activate that sensor is while choosing a teacher. Does this teacher have integrity? Does this teacher live what he or she teaches? Do you feel like he or she is accountable, respectful, connected to God, and do you feel you could trust this teacher?

When you first start working with your teachers, you will have to trust them at least somewhat to even ask them to teach you. (I speak of "teachers," rather than "teacher," because you may well have several teachers teaching you at a time, if you are in a spiritual school, or you may have several teachers instruct you over time.) You should not expect to feel as if you can immediately place your entire trust in your teachers. If the teachers have integrity, and you are willing to perceive it, your trust will develop over time. Many opportunities will arise as you work with these teachers that will give you a chance to find out how they handle things. Then you can decide how much you feel you can trust them. If you have found real teachers who have integrity and love, it will become apparent to you that you can trust those teachers not only with your physical life but also with the life of your eternal soul. When you know that to be true throughout your being, then you can truly be taught. For most people that takes some time. God is patient and will allow you the time you need.

Many people worry that if they submit to a teacher, they will be asked to do things they find unconscionable. What if the teacher told you that you had to kill someone, kill yourself, or abandon your children? This is a very common fear among people, often fueled by the stories of cults and cult leaders who have demanded such things of their followers. The answer is very simple: Any teacher who asks you to do something obviously immoral or wrong is in fact not in tune with God. Why would God ask you to break God's own laws? It is wrong to kill. It is wrong to not care for one's children. Why would God want our children to be abandoned? Does God not love them as much as God loves us? Why would God ask us through a teacher to take our own lives? Did not God give us this life and tell us in all the scriptures of all the religions that life is a holy gift to be respected and cared for?

I want to be extremely clear about this, because it is a great misconception that people have and that inspires much fear in many. You should *never* agree to do something a teacher tells you if it violates what you feel to be right or know to be true. I would like to add to that some very clear guidelines on the most often violated areas of trust between religious leaders and their followers: You should *never* be expected or even allowed to have a sexual relationship with your spiritual teacher. And you should *never* have to turn over all your money or all your possessions to them. Yes, it is true that the very early Christian communities that sprang up soon after Jesus left the Earth held all their possessions in common. Maybe, in extreme circumstances, that might be appropriate, or in communities that are set up to function that way. But in general, that should not be asked of a person.

First Judaism, then Christianity, set up a fair way of knowing what should be asked of members of spiritual groups to contribute to their spiritual communities. It is called "tithing." Members are asked to give 10 percent of their income to the place where they are spiritually fed. This is completely fair to all and allows spiritual communities to pay for the upkeep and care of the spaces and the ministers whose services they want and need. Churches will often ask for occasional additional monetary gifts for special projects, and some people choose to give more because they want to. But generally more is not required, which keeps individuals from feeling financially overburdened by their membership in a spiritual community.

Some people go to religious or spiritual centers and voice the opinion that one should not have to pay for spiritual services. The attitude is an interesting one for those of us who are providing the services and sometimes the sites for the services, too. We all know that it costs somebody money to maintain a space and give a lot of time for others to be able to come and receive wonderful spiritual training. When those coming to receive the services feel entitled to receive these services for free, they are actually saying that those providing the services should be carrying the burden of the expenses incurred. We hear this attitude over and over again at our centers where we are paying to lease or own a space, where we pay for all the utilities and supplies, the furnishings and food, and where the priests and deacons are donating their time as well as their money to keep it all running. Some students enter and say they feel that they should not have to pay for any of this if it is truly spiritual.

What causes us to feel that we should be fed for free? What do we mean by this? If we look carefully within ourselves, we will usually find several beliefs influencing us toward that attitude, such as, "I deserve to eat." This is spiritual food. If I make the effort to come people should take care of me; and anyone asking for my money must be trying to take advantage of me. (The attitudes are those of a child who is acting indignant that a parent would ask that they do their part.) If I am a child, no one should ask me to do anything but be there, right? Many people also feel their parents did not adequately give to them. That attitude is then projected onto this spiritual home, where the spiritual mom and dad should now finally give to this, their child, as they should have when they were young.

The second belief is that anyone who asks for our money must be trying to take advantage of us. Again, this is quite the consciousness, or lack of consciousness, of a child. In contrast to that, some students, upon entering our centers, note that, "It must take a good bit of money to keep such a place running. How and where can I contribute?" That demonstrates consciousness that someone must be paying to make these services available. These students want to make sure that they are doing their part. Those who see things this way have entered the adult world of taking responsibility and wanting to contribute their part to anything that is benefiting them. In so doing they demonstrate that they have understood a major aspect of the Law of Karma.

The Law of Karma is a Hindu teaching for which we don't have a particular word in English, so we have adopted their word. In Christian teachings, the Apostle Paul wrote in his letter to the Galations an explanation of the very essence of the Law of Karma. He said, "Whatever a person sows, that will they reap." And in the Gospel of Luke Jesus said, "For the measure you give, will be the measure you get back." That is the Law of Karma in a nutshell. It means that whatever we put out into the universe we will receive back. Whatever we do not pay for or are not willing to pay for is listed as a debt against us. When we truly understand this Law, we can see it as a great blessing and a great opportunity, rather than a curse. It states that we can influence and determine what comes to us by how and what we give.

Another cosmic principle exists that is often called the Principle or Law of Abundance. This principle states that an abundance of everything needed is present in the universe. We simply need to learn how to access it. This concept is a very important one for people to grasp, as it will change their lives once they do. God provides for us all through a flow of plenty of all that we need, and the way to receive abundantly is to let that flow move freely and fully. In order to get the flow going, we first need to make space in us to receive more. We make that space by letting go of something, giving something away. When we do that, we create a vacuum within our lives. Nature abhors a vacuum and will rush to fill it. We then experience that more of whatever we gave away comes back to us. If, on the other hand, we hold onto what we have out of fear that we will not have enough, our hand is a closed fist and we have no openness or space to receive more. We stop the flow of abundance to us. Then we remain in fear and in a state of scarcity.

A number of the top financial advisors in the Western Hemisphere have advocated that people learn to adopt the habit of giving if they truly want to thrive financially. When people do not have spiritual homes to which to give, these advisors tell them to give to other charities. Ten percent is the usual amount that is recommended. Many a fortune has been built on understanding this principle. If you also give to support the places that feed you spiritually, then you benefit from having those joyous attitudes in addition to having created the vacuum that must be filled. By giving, you state that you recognize that all that you have comes from God, that you are grateful to God for giving it all to you, and you believe God will continue to bless you. Then you will be drawing that blessing to you. This happens without fail, because it is a law of the universe, not just a nice idea.

What else is involved in becoming a spiritual student? We have discussed the need for trusting one's teachers, and for contributing one's fair share to where one is spiritually fed. In addition to those two requirements, a person wanting to enter into the life of being a spiritual student will have to implement the practice of placing God, and one's path to coming to know God, before all else in one's life. When you approach a teacher asking to be taught, you need to know that your spiritual training, like any other endeavor in life that requires much learning and practice, will need a good bit of your attention. You will need to spend time at the place you are learning to worship, meditate, and pray. You will need to spend time meeting with your teacher. You will also need to have times set aside at home for doing your spiritual practices. This is not something to enter into without an awareness and willingness to give the time needed to reach the goals you seek.

To a person that is not on the path, it may seem intrusive to let a teacher enter into and instruct all the aspects of a student's life, and yet students need to allow teachers to do so if they are to grow. Students may also feel very embarrassed when they begin to tell their teacher their most private indulgences, be they actions, thoughts, or feelings. It will feel intense to realize that your teacher sees right into you and that he or she can read you like a book. Soon enough, as one finds the courage to allow the teacher in, the student begins to experience the benefits of having a teacher. All the small and not-so-small things one previously would have worried about, struggled with, or stayed unclear about, are given the opportunity to be brought into consciousness. The student then gets to experience the blessing of having someone with clear spiritual sight peer into his or her life and give clarity and direction to that which was once scary and confusing.

In the early stages of the path, teachers will not usually tell students what they need to do. Much later, when students are farther in their spiritual growth, they may be given the opportunity to take vows, and one of the vows is that of obedience to the teacher. In the early stages of the work, the teachers are primarily supporting the students and helping them to see clearly what areas of their lives need work and how they might best approach those areas. If the teachers are skilled in dream interpretation, they may also work with the students' dreams. They may counsel students on how to improve their marriages, parenting, or careers. The students may need to take better care of their bodies or their finances, and the teachers may advise them accordingly. But the students are always free to do as they choose. The teachers are simply there to help and support.

Some teachers are also adept at using other methods to heal emotional and psychological wounds from which the students may be suffering. In our school, we administer memory healings when necessary. These memory healings can take students back into their pasts to when emotional or physical wounding occurred, and can bring healing into the memory itself. Such memory healings are very potent tools in the hands of a skilled teacher and can bring deep resolution and hence transformation into a person's life. Sometimes past-life regressions can help a student understand issues in this life that have previously not made sense. These also need to be done by someone who has sight and skill, and understands what is needed to bring about healing. Teachers can also transmit blessings, healings, and experiences of the heaven world and the beings in that world by laying their hands upon the students and allowing the power of God to move through them. All these methods and more are used to help the students clear up the things in their lives that are out of accord with harmony and truth, and to heal the wounds that bind them to the past. If the students are indeed willing and ready, nothing will be impossible for them to overcome as they place their feet upon the Path that leads to God.

The Stretch and Grow Effect of Spiritual Training on Marriage

Many people are surprised to learn what effect being on a spiritual path has on one's day-to-day life. As I began working with Master Peter, I believed that I would become so full of a high spiritual peace that my marriage would instantly become serene and wonderful and that Sal and I would be in bliss by just being together. All of our previous issues would surely dissolve in my new state of enlightenment, and he would be glad that I brought this light into our family and our life as a couple. He would, of course, want to join me on my path and we would have this blessed life of moving together into greater and greater light, love, and consciousness.

Things did not quite turn out that way. Sal was skeptical of my new spiritual school. He preferred the Sufi to the Christian approach, and he did not want to have a teacher. He felt that we were already overburdened with all the responsibilities that we were juggling without adding one more thing. Initially, I made the mistake of trying to tell him of all my great new understandings, insights, and experiences. I soon learned that he did not especially want to hear about them. I also felt a loss in myself when I told him about them, as if the experience was no longer so valuable in my own memory. I asked my teacher about this and I learned that this feeling of loss is common in such situations. When we share our spiritual experiences with someone other than our teacher, we will often feel as if we lose something of the blessing of we received. Talking about your spiritual growth with your mate may also stress your relationship, because he/she may feel that you are making yourself out to be better than him/her because you are now "becoming spiritual."

I had at this point quite seriously asked to be taught, not only by a teacher in a physical body, but also by the great Beings who are not in flesh bodies and who guide and teach those who are willing. Because I had entered into training with a real teacher, things started to happen in a much greater intensity in all the different parts of my life. Everything that was out of accord with divine harmony or divine truth was brought into sharp relief in my consciousness. The effect this had on my marriage is that everything that was wrong in our relationship surfaced. I was simultaneously shocked and thrilled by this—shocked, because it was hard to have to deal with our failures at communicating and loving each other, and thrilled because I knew I was being given an opportunity to learn to relate better and to love more deeply than I had known before.

Even though I was aware how beneficial all the new insights into our marital dysfunctions were, I still felt the pain of having to face our issues. The intensity of this work on my marriage was hard to bear at times. I finally had a spiritual teacher and an opportunity to delve into mystical teachings, yet I had to spend a great deal of my time talking with Master Peter about my marriage. I was frustrated. When I eventually saw that my work on my marriage *was* my work on my relationship with God, I felt more accepting of the relationship work and tried to be patient with myself. I also had to grieve the loss of the sweet illusion that my "becoming spiritual" was going to make for an easy everything: an easy marriage, an easy parenting experience, and an easy livelihood. I had to learn instead that I was bringing consciousness to every aspect of my life. As more divine light shone into my life from the center of light within me, more shadows showed up. Those cobwebs in the corners of my marriage, my parenting, my ability to keep a household, and my work as a midwife were all becoming obvious. I was embarrassed to let my teacher see all my shortcomings, and yet I knew that only what I confessed and addressed would be transformed. I did want to know God enough that it motivated me to confront my embarrassment and be honest about the problem areas in my life. As I did, I saw the growth that slowly permeated all of me and all that was mine. God's presence became apparent in all that I did, felt, and thought, and though it burned to feel seen by that pure presence and pure love in my nakedness, I knew I had to keep the faith and the courage if I was to be changed.

7

BY WATER AND BY FIRE: MYSTICAL BAPTISM AS THE FIRST INITIATION OF THE INNER PATH

Sleeper awake!
Rise from the dead,
And Christ will give you light.

—The Apostle Paul, *New Testament, Ephesians* 5:14

An Easter Morning Baptism

As I began my spiritual training with Master Peter and was learning about the mystical initiations, I thought back on my baptism, which I had been given on an Easter morning six years before meeting Master Peter. That had been my first mystical Christian initiation, so it seemed important to revisit it in mind and heart as I worked toward the second initiation. The baptism had taken place on a beautiful spring day. My recovery from anti-Christian sentiments was still in its early stages, so opening to spiritual experience in a Christian setting was very new to me. The Sisters at the Order Center had instructed me to do a retrospection of my life to see what wounds were yet unhealed and whether I still held resentments toward anyone. They told me that the baptism was not into any church, but was instead an initiation into a student-teacher relationship with Jesus Christ and Mother Mary. They said that in baptism I was asking for Jesus and Mary to take me on as one of their students and begin to lead me along the path toward illumination.

The morning began with a beautiful Easter service. I had just started to get a sense of a whole new way of understanding what the meaning of Jesus' crucifixion and resurrection might be. These kind and loving sisters helped me get a glimpse of how I might enter into the great mysteries of Jesus' death and subsequent rising from the dead, and how I might be transformed by the inner experience of those sacred events. On that Easter morning, I understood enough to feel very blessed to be receiving the initiation of baptism. The experience was intense. I felt as if the channel between God and I was opened on both ends, and I felt I had access to God, Jesus, and Mary as never before. The priest blessed my spiritual senses of perception and expression so that I might begin to see, hear, and feel more of the events occurring in the spiritual world, and that I might begin the process that over time would allow God's Truth to flow through my words. I felt that now I would perceive and express God more clearly in all my ways. I had a commitment to grow in my knowledge and expression of the truth.

From the moment of my baptism, my spiritual development began to accelerate. I could feel that the seed of light, which they said became ignited in a person at baptism, now in fact resided in me. I felt it drawing me toward the experiences and people I needed in order to grow. I had committed to God and to the Path of Jesus and Mary, and now I was being taught, stretched, and led by those greatest of master teachers themselves! All previous spiritual striving I had done through yoga seemed to have been child's play by comparison.

Preparation For and Entering Into Mystical Baptism

Baptism is the term Christianity uses for the first initiation on its inner path. Sufism, Zen, and Hasidism use other names, but the essential ingredients still need to be present for that first initiation, no matter the name, to function as a real starting point for the voyage to the God-Self at one's center. Before receiving this initiation, candidates must consider their pasts and take care of whatever karmic indebtedness remains. They will need to bring to consciousness any hurts they still hold against other people, as well as any guilt they still carry for their own mistakes and misdeeds. Candidates present these things to the teacher, and the teacher must know how to cleanse the students and heal them of their pasts so they can begin new lives.

Unless we have consciously searched for and expressed all the issues from the past that still disturb us, we remain carriers of our past and slaves to it. This retrospection is done as a form of confession in which the student knows that it is to his or her benefit to hide nothing. Anything not brought up for examination and purging will remain with them and will therefore bring pain and confusion whenever activated. Yes, students will have many more opportunities over the coming years of training to raise issues from the past. But why would anyone want to keep holding onto something that is painful if he or she has the opportunity to be free of it? The candidate is encouraged to offer as full a confession and communication as possible of his or her past hurts and guilt.

In the Order of Christ/Sophia, the students do the retrospection in three weeks. Obviously, not everything from someone's past will be addressed over a three-week period, yet an amazing amount of pain does come up and is healed during this short time. The students are often astonished at the power of this intensive look into themselves. They are told to ask Jesus and Mary to assist them in finding what they need to look at in their pasts and what they need to share with their teachers. This adds an immense power to the retrospection and helps the student find those life experiences that are of greatest importance to address at that time.

Everybody's life story contains times when they felt unloved and misunderstood. Most people also feel that they were at least somewhat abused: some sexually, some physically, and some emotionally. We all find different ways to cope with our childhood wounds. Very few people, however, have actually healed those wounds completely. When students tell us that they had a happy childhood and nothing painful happened to them, we look to see if they have merely buried the pain or whether they actually grew up pain free. Those who buried the pain and believe they have none ignored what was hurtful around them and only noticed or remembered what was nice. This coping mechanism works well for many to get them going in life. However, at some time, the hurt and fear that they have not acknowledged will begin to surface, often in confounding ways. Then the student tends to need to get help to figure out what is going on.

None of us grow up without doing some things wrong. Sometimes we knew at the time that what we were doing was wrong; other times we recognized it later. When we examine these mistakes, we realize that they were hurtful and sometimes even harmful to others, often carrying potential long-term consequences. We often feel badly about what we have done to others and ourselves, but do not know what we can do to change the situations. Some people bury all these memories, too, or rationalize why they do not feel badly about their misdeeds. They allow their thinking to declare that they did not mean harm or were too young to know, and then they assume the issue is closed. Often their feelings of guilt have simply been repressed. When people do this, they tend to get angrier over the years as those repressed feelings rebel for lack of acknowledgement. Eventually, these unacknowledged feelings come up, often in disguised forms, and the people are dumfounded as to what is causing the intense feelings that rise up inside of them.

Humans don't do well in the long-term if they do not acknowledge past feelings of hurt, guilt, and shame and bring healing into those memories and feelings. Baptism gives us a chance to start anew as we begin a conscious spiritual path. This is a perfect time to clean up the leftover pain of the past. Baptism carries additional power when one has access to a priest who can actually lift the karmic debt for the person's mistakes and wrongdoings right off of his or her soul. In Christian terminology, that lifting of karmic debt is called the "absolution," or "absolving" of sins. Many people have a negative reaction to the word "sin," often because they feel they have been beaten up with it. For others it just does not make sense or seem useful to have such a term. Coming from a conservative Christian upbringing I had much resistance to any conversation about sin. I was greatly helped to make peace with the concept of sin once the Sisters explained it to me from the mystical perspective. The word "sin" actually comes from a Greek word that means "missing the mark." No matter how good we may try to be, sometimes we miss the mark. When we do, we incur a karmic debt, which means our souls carry a record of that wrong for as long as it remains unresolved. As with accounting balance sheets, when there is a debit, it can only be erased by an equal credit to the account. The way we can erase debits on our souls is to go back to that situation and make it right, or we can have the error absolved, or forgiven, by God.

The priest can play a powerful role in this process. Many times people want to know if they are forgiven but do not feel they can make a clear enough contact with God to be certain. With ordination, priests are given the power to bind things to a person's soul or free the person from them. In Matthew 16:19 Jesus said, speaking to the Apostle Peter as the first of His priests, "Whatever you bind on earth will be bound in heaven, and whatever you loose on earth will be loosed in heaven." This is the power given to priests who work under the Master Jesus. A true priest will have the spiritual sight to know what a person needs to see and understand about his or her past errors. In order to have an error lifted, we need to look deeply into ourselves and see why we made that error. We need to look at what we got out of it and what the consequences were, both to us and to other people. When we have seen all that and have felt the damage we did, we need to resolve never to do that again. Then we are ready to be forgiven.

When people ask for forgiveness without having explored the roots of why they indulged in that particular misdeed, they often find themselves repeating mistakes. The unconscious motives must be made conscious. Any possible reparations for those misdeeds that still can be done often need to be done. Forgiveness and absolution were not meant to be ways people could keep feeling good about doing wrong. They were meant to clear the slate once people were ready to change. When we are ready to change, it is a great blessing to have the past wiped clean so that we can start anew. It took me many years to understand what an immense gift we were given by the Master Jesus when he provided us with a means to have our sins forgiven. As a teacher, I speak with people daily who come to me burdened with guilt and shame. After they confess their errors, recognize how those errors came about, and resolve not to replicate the mistakes, I give them absolution. They leave feeling a huge burden has been lifted from them. Psychotherapy does not have the power and gift of absolution to offer people, and people in the care of psychotherapists often revisit their guilt and shame for numerous years attempting to feel free of those feelings, sometimes never achieving that goal.

After candidates are thoroughly prepared by doing the life retrospection and have been absolved of their past errors, they are ready to be baptized. In the baptism sacrament of the Order of Christ/Sophia, the candidate is anointed with oil that has been blessed for this purpose. Olive oil has from ancient times been said to be a good conductor of cosmic rays and of the higher energies. In the Psalms, King David spoke of having his head anointed with oil. The anointing prepares the candidates to receive the blessing that will be called down. The candidates are asked whether they feel ready to enter into this initiation. If a last-minute issue comes up that the initiate feels is unresolved, then the baptism is put on hold while the candidate speaks with the priest or minister to resolve the troublesome thought or feeling. Once the candidate is ready, the minister/priest lays hands on the candidate's head and begins to bring the light into that person, calling down the consciousness and power of God. The power of this calling down resonates through the sanctuary. Whenever I observe mystical baptisms being performed, I feel the sound of those words shaking me to the core. The power of God descends and moves into the candidate. Inside each person resides a place that awaits the descent of such a power to ignite a small flame. This flame, once lit, fires up the gift of spiritual Sight that we all have lying dormant within us. It also begins the potential to grow the inner light.

Practicing Midwifery and The Man Who Did Not Want a Daughter

As baptism launches the beginning of a new, spiritually guided life, one who has been baptized may find that soon afterward, many aspects of his or her life become clearer. One of the things I began to see and know shortly after my baptism was that I was to work with women having babies. This became an important part of my life's work. At the time, there was no home-birth movement in Kentucky, where I was living. I also had no one with whom to train, as no one else in the area was attending home births. The skills needed are often specific to the birth location, which is in a woman's home. The first birth I was asked to attend was a do-it-yourself birth, like our son Nathan's had been. The mother giving birth became my midwifery partner. We knew next to nothing in those early days of home birthing. We studied and learned from anyone we could, from labor and delivery nurses to friendly obstetricians to midwives in other states who counseled us over the phone. We knew that only by the assistance of the spiritual world did we have the good outcomes we did, which consisted of healthy and happy mothers and babies.

I found truth in the popular saying, "God helps those who help themselves." Over and over I learned about a certain complication or how to handle a certain situation, and within a week or two I was confronted with it. I developed a certain belief that as long as I did everything in my power to keep learning and growing in my midwifery skills and knowledge, God would cover the areas where I was still lacking. Over the next 24 years, I attended over 600 home births and a few hundred hospital births. At some time or another, I experienced most everything that can go wrong in pregnancy and birth. Through the protection of the heavenly hosts and applying all that we learned, we pulled through even harrowing experiences feeling we had provided care that was as good as what could be given under the circumstances.

The ways I found myself receiving what I needed to know were often astonishing. Sometimes my midwifery partner, Nancy, and I called the authors of textbooks to ask them what they meant on a certain page or how to do a particular procedure. We found a family doctor who was also a Catholic nun. She considered her duty to God to include helping us any way she could. Her fellow doctors were quite displeased that she was assisting us in our practice. When they confronted her, she told them that she answered to a higher authority—God—and that her commitment was to helping those who needed help. Who needed help more than those whom no one else would agree to help? So when clients needed a few stitches after giving birth, she came to their homes to suture them and to teach us how to suture. She agreed to see our clients in the hospital when we needed to transport them for various complications. She was even present at my second daughter's home birth, as a spectator only, because she wanted to see a midwife-attended home birth.

The Kentucky laws applicable to practicing midwifery stated that if one went to the Health Department and registered as a midwife, one would be issued a license or permit to practice. These were old laws that pertained to the granny midwives of times past. But they had not been changed and therefore should have pertained to the new kind of midwifery that we were practicing. The Health Department refused to issue any new licenses. This left us practicing midwifery without a license, which was not a situation we relished. We could conceivably be brought up on criminal charges, and even serve prison terms. We heard of this happening to some midwives in other states. So we had to be careful about getting caught by anyone who might wish us harm. Over the next two years, Nancy and I worked intensively to change the laws that regulated midwifery as an independent profession. At the end of the two years, having failed to bring about change through the judicial, legislative, or executive branches of our state government, we gave up the effort. We had learned a lot about government and its corruption, and I felt burned out and done with that chapter of my life.

When a woman is giving birth, she is at the portal between life and death. Most women are keenly aware of that. Much of the mystery and the fear around birth exists because it cannot be approached without the knowledge that one may also be headed for an experience of death, either that of the mother or the baby. When a couple chooses to give birth at home, they generally do so after having read that the statistics of outcomes for home and hospital birth are equal. They choose to enter into this experience in an environment in which there will be no opportunity to obtain pain medication. These mothers know that it would be very hard to not accept pain medication once they are in the throes of labor. So they choose in advance, before labor, when their judgment, strength, and courage are not compromised, to give birth where they will not be tempted to accept the narcotics hospitals' offer. Many also make the home birth choice because of the sense that birth is a sacred event, and they want to experience it where they have more control over their environment. They can maintain the feeling of sacredness better at home than if they were in an institution such as a hospital.

The subject of souls, how they come into incarnation, and how they come to be with their parents, is also paramount to birth. A yet little-known field of study called Perinatal Psychology deals with how babies are affected by what goes on *in utero*, during birth, and during the time shortly thereafter. If we acknowledge that babies are not deaf, blind, or dumb, and that they are most certainly not insensitive to what is happening around them after birth, why would we think they are insensitive before birth? Most people fail to realize that newborns are not stupid but can simply not yet use their bodies to communicate. They hear and feel extremely clearly, and they understand language and emotions around them quite well, for they have lived many lives. They need time to settle into the new vehicles, i.e. their bodies, before they can communicate to us what they know and how much they understand.

When I practiced midwifery in Kentucky, I also taught home birth classes that my clients were required to attend. I wanted them to be well versed in what to expect, and I wanted them to have a basic understanding of what could go wrong and what we would need to do if something did happen. So my clients tended to be extremely well-informed about normal and complicated birth.

The husband of one of my clients only came to classes because he had to. He was what is often referred to as a "redneck." We will call this burly redheaded fellow Bob. Bob worked a blue-collar job and loved beer and football. He and his wife, Debbie, had two girls. During the first class, Bob told the other couples present that he loved his girls but that *this* kid *had* to be a boy. He wanted a son, and he would not hear of having another daughter.

During the prenatal classes, I encouraged the expectant parents to become aware of that little person inside the mother, how the baby perceived what they said, and how they felt about him or her. I explained how the mother is the baby's entire environment. If she is unhappy about having the baby or constantly worried, it is the same as if for you the walls of the room around you, the air you breathe, the sounds you hear, and the feelings you feel, were all unhappy with your existence or worried about whether you were okay. I hoped to raise the parents' consciousness to take the baby into account as a real person, not just as a not-yet-human creature. I told them to talk to the baby inside, to pay attention to it, and to let it know how welcome it was and how much they looked forward to meeting it face to face.

Bob pulled me aside after that particular class and told me that he respected me as a midwife and as a person, but that he just could not accept this garbage about talking to the baby inside his wife's belly. He thought this was ludicrous, and he said he needed me to know he could not go along with such things. A few weeks later, I went to their house for the prenatal home visit. His wife had been telling me all along how worried she was about what Bob would do if this baby were to be a girl. As we talked, two neighbors came over and told me that they were also extremely worried about how Bob would deal with another daughter. His emphatic statements about how this *had* to be a boy seemed to have the whole neighborhood concerned. Bob would hear nothing of it when I tried to talk with him about it. He said that it wasn't an issue because he, in fact, intuitively knew that it *was* a boy, so all would be fine.

Debbie's due date came and went. We had a deadline of two weeks past due date, after which we sent our clients who had not yet given birth to the hospital to be induced. When Debbie reached that date, she was very upset at the prospect of having to give up her planned home birth. Her cervix was four centimeters dilated and felt very ready to give birth. All she needed was contractions. But she had none. I went to their house to discuss their options with them. Bob was also disappointed that their planned home birth seemed to be a diminishing prospect. He came to me while I took notes in their living room and asked me what they could do to stimulate labor. They had already done all the herbal and natural remedies that often work to trigger contractions, to no avail. I said to him, "There is something else that might work, but I don't think you want to hear about it."

He said, "Yes I do. Please tell me. Anything!"

I replied, "Bob, if you were your wife, and you suspected that you were carrying a baby girl, would you want to give birth?"

Bob jumped up in protest. "Oh, come on now! You are not saying that my wife is not going into labor because she is afraid of having a girl? She knows I would love a girl if we had one!"

"She does?" I asked. "*I* don't know that. Why would she? Have you told her that?"

"That is ridiculous! Debbie!" he called, heading toward the kitchen where she was. I listened in as I heard him say, "Debbie, you know I would love a girl, don't you? Of course I want a boy, but I love our two daughters. Why would I not love another one?"

Debbie broke into tears and told him that she in fact had not been sure that he would love another daughter. He held her, comforted her, and said that all would be fine. He then came back in the living room and said, "Are you happy now?"

I said, "Well, there is someone else who may not know that it would be okay to be a girl."

"The baby? You want me to talk to the baby?! You *must* be kidding!"

"I told you that you wouldn't want to hear what I had to say. I am simply telling you that if I was that baby and I knew I was a girl, I don't think I would want to come out."

Bob paced incredulously up and down the floor mumbling about how babies don't hear or think when they are inside, and how silly this conversation was. Then he said, "I think it is ridiculous, but if there is any chance at all that it will make a difference, then I will do it." He went back into the kitchen and I heard him speaking to his wife's belly, "Baby, I feel this is really stupid. But I don't want to be the one who didn't do everything in his power to help you have a home birth, so I am talking to you. I know that you aren't silly like these other people. You do know that I will love you even if you are a girl. Yes, I *really* want a son, but how could I not love a daughter of mine. Okay?"

He returned to the living room with his jacket swung over his shoulder. "Are you satisfied? This ridiculous talk has stressed me out. I'm going to the bar up at the corner. Call me if you need me!"

Bob left. Nancy, Debbie, and I sat down and had a good laugh. Debbie was also teary with relief after so many months of worry and fear about having another daughter and Bob rejecting the baby. Within a half hour, Debbie had her first contraction, and her labor moved quickly into high gear. We called the bar to get Bob back home. Forty minutes after the first contraction, a beautiful red-haired little girl was born into Bob's and my waiting hands. The labor had gone perfectly, but this little girl was not breathing. As I began all the usual stimulation to get her going, I handed her to Bob and said, "I think this is between you and her."

He held her right there with one hand under her back and head and the other on her chest, while I suctioned her, flicked her feet, rubbed her back, and gave her some oxygen. Bob started talking to her. "Hi, Baby! Hey, Baby, why aren't you breathing? Don't you want to be here? You aren't thinking that I don't want you because you are a girl, are you? You can't be believing *that*! You must know, I am all talk. Have you seen how I love your sisters? You are beautiful! How could I not love you?"

After a couple of minutes ticked by and the baby still failed to breathe, Bob became desperate. Tears dropped from his eyes onto the little girl. "*Please*, Baby! *Please* breathe! I am so sorry if I made you feel unwanted! I am *so* sorry! *Please* breathe!" At this, the little girl opened her eyes and looked straight at her father. Still not breathing, her look seemed to say, "Are you for real?"

The intensity of Bob's pleading doubled. He wept and pleaded until the baby took a breath. Because he was holding her, he felt that first breath between his hands. He cried out, "She's breathing! She's breathing!"

I told him to just keep talking to her while I continued doing my job. The little girl's breaths came more regularly as Bob continued to weep and tell her of his love. When the baby was stable, Bob wrapped her in a blanket, and much to all of our surprise, he walked out of the room with her in his arms. Debbie was upset. "Where is he taking my baby? I haven't even held her yet!"

I went out looking for Bob and the baby. The front door was open. I was now quite concerned about what he was up to. It was a hot summer day. I found Bob standing out in the middle of the street of this suburban subdivision holding the baby up toward the heavens and crying out at the top of his voice, "I have a baby girl, and I love her!"

The neighbors were coming out of their houses. I ran over to Bob and told him that the baby really needed to be with her mother now. He complied, though when he handed her to Debbie, he acted as if she was his baby and Debbie needed his instruction and supervision. The baby looked just like Bob. By what we had witnessed, it sure seemed like she had been unsure of whether to come into that body and claim it if Dad did not welcome her. She wanted him to be very clear about that before she made her commitment. Over the months that followed, I saw her become the apple of his eye. A year or so later, I heard from Debbie that Bob now seemed unable to recall any of the above events ever having taken place. It was so incongruent with the rest of what he held to be true and how he lived, that he wiped it out of his memory banks. However, his wife, his midwives, and his neighbors knew. And Bob's love for that little girl seemed to be sealed for life.

The Prayer of a Orthodox Jewish Woman Giving Birth

I prayed on my way to attend women in labor. I often prayed during their labor, quietly, to myself. Over and over, I felt the presence of Mother Mary at births. I often felt her even if the parents were not spiritual or open to her. When a mother *was* open to her and called on her or prayed to her in labor, Mary's presence filled the place and brought peace and a sense of heaven to the birth rooms. I had clients of all religions and clients of no religion. One day, I attended the birth of a Hasidic Jewish woman. She had actually wanted to go to the hospital, but her labor was progressing too quickly, so I agreed to attend her right there at home. She had been afraid that she would not be able to stand the pain and wanted to be where she could get an epidural. But now the baby was coming, and there was no time to go to the hospital.

Having worked with many Hasidic families, I knew that Hasidic men are not supposed to see their wives' genitals. In the past, I had found ways to respect this wish while birthing at home. When it became obvious that the three of us were alone for the birth, the woman turned to her husband and said a Hebrew word to him. She then told me it meant that this was an emergency and all rules were off. He would assist me in whatever way I needed. The baby moved very quickly to the point of crowning. This is when the largest part of the baby's head is about to emerge. It is a very intense time for most women. I told the mother that this was the hardest moment for her, and it would be over very soon. When she heard me say it was the hardest moment, she turned to her husband and said, "This is the time! We must pray now!" By her sheer will, she seemed to stop the next contraction from coming, while she and her husband prayed a detailed prayer for peace in Israel and for many other people and situations, but no prayers for themselves. As soon as they were done, she gave a push, and the baby came out.

After the birth, I asked them what that was all about. The mom told me that there is a Jewish teaching that prayers for other people offered when one is in intense pain or difficulty carry special blessings and power. She said she wanted to make sure to not miss that opportunity to give such blessings to others. I was highly impressed and deeply moved. Never have I forgotten what I learned that day, and through the years I have come to know how true it is. If people will only care about others and pray for them when they themselves are in dire need, they will not only find their prayers carry extra power and blessing, but they themselves will feel better. When we take our thoughts off ourselves, we give God a chance to take care of us, heal our wounds, and grant us all that we need. This can be done in much more ordinary moments in life than the moment of birth. It is a practice I do myself and encourage all to undertake. If you are lying awake at night worried about something, get up and pray for five people. You will feel amazingly relieved of your worry or preoccupation, and if the five people are open to it, so will they feel the relief brought to them by your prayers. If you are in physical pain, pray for others. If you are anxious or depressed, pray for others and you will be healed. The act of caring about others in and of itself brings healing power into every aspect of our lives.

8

THE SEALING OF THE LIGHT: ILLUMINATION AS THE SECOND INITIATION OF THE INNER PATH

The light of the body is the eye. Therefore when your eye is single, your whole body also is full of light…If your whole body therefore is full of light, having no part dark, the whole will be full of light, as when the shining of a candle gives you light.

—Jesus, *Luke 11: 34 & 36*

Winter Solstice and Receiving the Initiation of Illumination

Master Peter had been teaching me for a number of months. I was learning an immense amount through the esoteric and mystical lessons he gave me to study. I began to understand how to be a spiritual student. In addition, my inner world of Spirit was changing, sometimes almost imperceptibly to me, and at other times overwhelming me with experiences of a spiritual nature. My spiritual sight was getting clearer. I could see more within my being and into what one might call "the heaven world," which is usually unseen to those who use only their physical eyes. As I recounted my spiritual visions and experiences to my teacher, with his assistance I learned to distinguish between my accurate perceptions in the spiritual realm from those that were my own creations. I came to appreciate the extraordinary opportunity I had to have someone with clear spiritual sight review my visions and perceptions with me and confirm or question them.

As my spiritual life intensified, I also became more aware of all the inharmonious parts of my life. My marriage was going through a big shakeup and resorting of how we related. At this point, we had four children and lived on our homestead farm in rural Kentucky. Sal and I had some of our most difficult disputes during this time. I did not understand why our marriage seemed so challenging. With my current perspective and knowledge, I know that often when one partner is growing rapidly and changing in various ways, the other partner can feel quite threatened. Later I saw that Sal was wondering whether I would still love him and want to stay with him if I became highly spiritual. He also felt uncomfortable about my springing ahead of him in spiritual development, and seemed to want to prove that he could still get me emotionally off balance on a daily basis.

The night described at the beginning of this book, in which I became so angry at him, was during this period. My visit to Master Peter's house the next day was to attend a class that was to be followed by the Winter Solstice Service. It was December 21, and my midwifery partner, Nancy, came with me. During the class, I felt lifted up into the spiritual realms to such an extent that I could hardly keep my grounding. I asked Master Peter whether Mother Mary and the Master Jesus did something different at this time of year, because I felt Mother Mary so very close and present but did not feel Jesus as much. Master Peter smiled and told me it was, in fact, just as I said. Jesus would be coming forth at Christmas; now it was Mary's time. I was glad to have my experiences of Jesus' and Mary's whereabouts confirmed because I had, in fact, been feeling Mary everywhere. Whenever I closed my eyes, I felt her right there, all around me. Contacting her was easy and through these contacts with Her I felt that I was beginning to get to know her and what her mission and work was—2,000 years ago and now.

After the class, Master Peter opened the doors to the small chapel that was in his house. About 12 people were in attendance. With candles lit and the lights dimmed, the solstice service began. Master Peter explained why we celebrate the solstices and equinoxes. They are the times of the year when we acknowledge being a part of our solar system and when we can open to the heavenly hosts who are looking toward the sun and our planet's relationship to the sun. The winter solstice occurs when, after six months of the days getting ever shorter, they once again begin to lengthen. It is therefore seen as the day of the coming forth of the sun. Many of the great teachers or avatars are said to have been born on the winter solstice. That day also begins the astrological sign of Capricorn, which is the sign of the teacher. Those avatars and teachers who were born on that day are like suns being born for the earth, and are said to bring great light. We celebrate Jesus' birth three days later. Some say that this was simply an error, and that he was born on the solstice. Others say that it takes three days for a solar event, like a solstice, to actually come into the earth consciousness, and therefore he was born into the earth three days later.

My experience of the solstice service was that it was hardly of the earth, and more of heaven. I could not make out what any of it meant with my conscious mind, but I felt the service lift me into another reality. I sensed the presence of great beings of light all around us. At the end of the solstice service, I was kneeling at one end of a long row of celebrants when Master Peter asked me to come up and kneel near the altar. I had never been to a solstice service before, so I thought this was a continuation of it. I imagined that I would be the first to go up, and then all the others would, too, one by one. Master Peter placed his hands on my head as I knelt, and I felt an enormous amount of energy and light come down on me. He kept working on me in various ways. After a while, he asked me whether I knew what was happening. I was astonished, saying that I assumed we were still doing the solstice service. He laughed and told me that I was being brought into the initiation of illumination. He continued to work on increasing the intensity of the light in me until it filled my whole body. Master Peter asked another teacher who was present to confirm that she saw my whole body fill with light, too. He concluded the initiation by pronouncing the sealing of that light within my body.

Master Peter asked me if I would like to sleep in the chapel that night. I was delighted. I could not imagine a more wonderful place to sleep. As I rose and moved around, I was amazed at the intensity of what was happening in my body and mind. I had trouble knowing where my body ended and the energy field around it began. I found my mind perfectly still and filled with a bright and harmonious consciousness. I slept a little and laid awake a lot. Each time I woke up, I found that the intensity of the light in my body had increased even more. I felt awed and amazed at what had been given to me—and how real and indisputable it was.

When I woke in the morning, I could hardly speak. Walking felt strange because I wasn't sure where my body began and ended. Master Peter laughed at my confusion about these sensations and explained to me that every cell in my body had now taken on that light, and it was permanently sealed into the cells. I was given a new baseline from which to grow. He told me that this was an initiation, not a completion. In other words, I had begun, not finished, this work of becoming a being full of light. Initiations open the door to us and allow us to begin the next phase of a journey. They do not mean that we are all done with a given stage. Master Peter gave me spiritual exercises. He told me to do them intensively over the next 30 days to help me learn to work with what had been given to me, and to help me develop a relationship with it.

I was glad for my friend Nancy's presence because I wasn't sure I could drive responsibly. Once home, I took time to reintegrate into my life with the four kids, Sal, the farm, and the midwifery calls. I told Sal in very general terms that I had been initiated. Master Peter had warned me to not say much, as Sal could not possibly know what I was describing, and therefore could not appreciate it. Over the following days, each morning when I awoke, I was amazed to find the light still with me. I thought about how moods and feelings often don't stay with us after a night's sleep. Therefore, this experience had to be something different from a mood or feeling. It was not dependent on my thinking about it or concentrating on it. It had its own existence within me, no matter what else I was doing, thinking, or feeling. When I did sit and meditate, the light became even brighter, but it never went away.

I not only saw the light, but also felt it as a sensation in my body. Additionally, a stillness and peace accompanied it and filled my mind and heart. It amazed me as a completely indisputable reality. I had to rethink everything I had always held to be real. Master Peter instructed me to be aware of carrying that light in everything I did. When I wiped down the kitchen counter, I tried to be aware that I was spreading light across it. When I walked and talked, I sought to let that light work in and through me. My heart overflowed with gratitude to God, Jesus, and Mary, to this spiritual school, and to my teacher. What grace that I had been given such a gift and had truly entered upon the Path to God! I was keenly aware that I had done nothing that could warrant my receiving such a gift. Only through God's Love and Grace was this given to me.

Illumination and Difficulty with Accepting Jesus and Mary

The initiation of illumination is not simply a nice experience that makes people feel good about themselves and God. It is an essential step on the path to coming to meet God at the center of one's being. Yes, a few people throughout history have had this step given to them by a teacher from the unseen realms. Some have also received it from Jesus or Mary directly, but those people are few and far between. People who received their initiations through teachers from the unseen realms were generally living lives of extreme sacrifice and devotion and had no one in human form to help them move beyond the accomplishments of their spiritual discipline. God had mercy on them and brought them into His/Her light. The point is that when there was no initiation, priests, and teachers to give the illumination, few people could come into this experience. The extreme sacrifices and devotions that the saints of old practiced engendered the help of discarnate teachers who came to assist these great devotees into the consciousness and knowledge of God. However, through the initiations, almost anyone will be able to come into this experience within three months to two years after beginning to prepare for it. One seeking to come into the illumination will have to find a teacher to guide him or her and do the work to empty out much of the anger, hurt, sadness, and self-centeredness he or she has held inside. They will then need to let that teacher or priest teach them how to build up the light within them, and allow themselves to be filled with the presence of God. Finally, they need a priest or teacher who knows how to bring them into that initiation and who was given the authority by his or her own teacher to perform this sacrament.

If you have developed some spiritual sight you can actually see how certain people carry light. The halos painted around many of the saints' pictures are indicative of the light they gave off. The New Testament tells us that when Jesus went through the transfiguration on the mountaintop, he shone so brightly that the three apostles who were with him had to hide their faces. In the New Testament, we are also told that when the first deacon, Stephen, was stoned to death, even those who were stoning him found that he shone so intensely, they were blinded by the light.

Jesus said, "If your eye is single, your whole body will be filled with light." What did he mean by saying one's eye would need to be single? Before students of the inner path are brought through the initiation of illumination, they must sacrifice some activities in their lives that require too much of their attention. They must have placed all their intention on wanting God, which is what Jesus meant by one's "eye being single." That is not as extreme as it may sound. In the Order of Christ/Sophia, everyone continues to go to work, attend school, or care for their children. They still go to movies, eat out, and enjoy life, but they will have to make some real changes before they are brought into this initiation. These changes are focused around what they value and how much attachment they have to those inner or outer aspects of their lives. They must allow their teachers to help them examine their emotional holdings, and they must do some significant examining of all the thought patterns that have kept them stuck. They also have to make coming into a real relationship with God of primary importance in their lives. They need to develop humility and openness to God, Jesus, and Mary, through whom we are able to offer these initiations. You may now see how the inner spiritual path and the way of initiation is not for everyone. It is not meant to be for all, rather only for those who feel that finding and experiencing God and entering into their mission in this life is of paramount importance.

Some people have asked me, "What if I want all these teachings and I want to come into these experiences and initiations, but I don't want to have to accept Jesus and Mary? I am not interested in working with them."

This does come up periodically from people who for various reasons are opposed to opening to these two beings. My question back to such a person might be: "What have you got against them?"

They usually respond with a form of, "I just don't feel a desire to deal with anything Christian, and I don't believe that one should have to go through any particular beings to get to God."

I might then ask back, "How do you know?"

They say, "It is just how I feel, what I believe."

I would respond, "What if God actually decided to put a particular pair of people in charge of this planet? Do you believe God has a right to make such a decision?"

The stubborn ones say, "I don't think there should be just one way."

"I didn't say there was one way. One can also take the Sufi, Kabballah, or Zen paths and reach the same endpoint. What if God decided He/She wanted all the paths to come under a particular Master or two? Do you grant that God has the right to do so?" This begins to stump most people. "Would you care to find out how God wanted it to be and how God set it up? Would you be open to finding out that God, in fact, made Jesus and Mary world saviors if that is actually the way it is? Or would you not want to know and would you not accept it even if that was what God had decided?"

What I am after in such inquiries with potential students is whether they are humble enough to want to know how God would like for us to see our world and how God would like for us to work with Him/Her. Or are they so proud that they see themselves as above God? Do they think they have superior knowledge that allows them to know that Jesus and Mary would actually be a bad choice for being in charge of the further development of this planet? If they have such pride and no openness to finding out the truth for themselves, then I know they are not good candidates for the inner path. They are, in fact, more wed to their own opinions than to finding out the truth, and they have a wall blocking them from any truth they happen to have a bias against. This would prevent them from allowing God to lead them, teach them, and transform them into beings of light.

On the other hand, if someone simply has no experience with Jesus and Mary and does not know who they really are and what role they play for the Earth, but is willing to find out, then that person is a fine candidate for the path. By being humble and open, it won't be too long before this student starts to have spiritual experiences and comes to know these beings. As the student experiences what great love and healing power is available by opening to Jesus and Mary, he or she becomes a firsthand witness to why it is so helpful and wonderful to allow these greatest lovers of humankind to pour their healing love into us. Humility toward God and His/Her choices is one of the most essential qualities in a student of the truth. The greater the humility, dedication, and simplicity, the greater the growth and the faster the development will be to union with God.

Some people get upset that God did not consult them when He/She was deciding what was best for this planet. God did not invite all the souls to come and vote for who was to be the Lord of Earth. God instead gave the job to those who were most likely to be able to endure the immense job of taking on the sins (the karma) of the whole planet and change its course from one headed for destruction to one headed toward transformation. Jesus and Mary volunteered for the job and were given it because they were the most capable. If we are offended that we were not consulted on this, then we show how very far we are from understanding and knowing anything about God. We are still lost in thinking that we are the center of all and nothing should move without our wanting it. This would be an indicator that we need a bit more time to be lost in the ways of the world, because we are not yet tired of it and of ourselves. After more painful experiences, we may find that our pride has been shattered and we are more prepared to approach God in a humble and simple way.

Personally, if I was to be with Jesus or Mary in prayer or meditation, and they took me to a being and said, "I want you to meet my teacher," and they then introduced me to Buddha, Mohammed, or Moses, or for that matter anyone else, I would say, "Thank you so much. I am so glad to meet you and to know that you are my teacher's teacher. I would like to know you better." If students can be that open to finding out who's who in the spiritual world, they will be fine. If they have a blockage to finding out, they are not yet ready for the spiritual path.

For people to come into the initiation of illumination they will, therefore, have had to move past all the barriers in their minds that prevent them from opening to the spiritual world. They need to have gained the humility to allow things to be as God decided they should be, even if that is not how the student would have chosen. Without such humility, as well as dedication to the path and trust in the teacher, it is not possible to truly accept the great light into one's being, and begin to become a being of light as well.

One of the benefits of having the light sealed within one's body, as is done in the initiation of illumination, is that you can then go through all of life's experiences with more consciousness of the world that you see with the physical eyes versus the world that you see with the spiritual eyes. A person within whom the light has been sealed can therefore obtain an understanding of events in his or her life from the regular point of view of humans on Earth, as well as from the point of view of the higher realms of existence.

The following story tells of a major event in my life that I experienced only months after being illumined. It is an example of how the light in my being allowed me to enter into an understanding that transformed my experience of this event and greatly enhanced the wisdom I could gain from it. If I had not been working on developing my spiritual sight and my ability to perceive events and beings in the heaven worlds, it is not likely that I would have been able to perceive the being that came to me at the end of the story, from whom I learned so much. The light in me increased my sight into those worlds just as turning on a light in a room allows one to see what is there.

A Miscarriage, and the Appearance and Conversation with the Lost Baby's Soul

One morning, as I was praying at my shrine, Mother Mary spoke to me and told me I was pregnant. This was my sixth pregnancy. Two years earlier, I had given birth to our third daughter, Sofia, there in the house Sal had built for us way out in the Kentucky countryside. We were all excited about this new pregnancy. Nathan was hoping to finally get a brother. Sofia was glad that she would no longer be the youngest. Odessa and Pascale were looking forward to having a baby to play with and dress up. Sal and I were happy to have another child coming to join our family. We had already agreed that this one, if a boy, would be named Francesco, after Sal's deceased father.

During my fifth month, I was expecting to feel the baby move any day. Instead, one morning, I felt my water break. I got my ultrasonic stethoscope out to listen for the baby's heart tones. Where there should have been a happy heartbeat emitting from my uterus, there was instead a deadly silence. I tried to not jump to conclusions before having someone else check my belly. I called Nancy and asked her to come over and check for any signs of life coming from inside of me. After a long, increasingly emotional listening session, she confirmed that she could not hear any heart tones. With great sadness, I had to accept that this baby was no longer alive. My sadness felt interior, personal, and quiet rather than external. Sal was deeply distressed when I told him the news. We both saw the dreams we had for this little one shatter and disappear. No new baby would be joining our family four months later, as we had been hoping. I was already staring to cramp, so I knew my body was doing its job and was kicking me into labor to give birth to what would now be an ending of a relationship, instead of a beginning of one. Though I felt profound sorrow, I also knew I had to be practical and prepare for my labor and birth. Nancy and I hugged a teary hug. She offered to take my four kids to her house so that I could labor and grieve in peace. I gratefully accepted her help. Sal and I were left to the sad task of waiting for what would be a birth and a death experience all wrapped into one.

This turned out to be my longest labor. My body was completely unprepared to give birth. The labor lasted a full three days. Since the baby did not need monitoring because it was no longer living, and I felt like I wanted to be by myself to pray and be with Mother Mary, I turned down the offers of the other midwives in the area to come assist me. I told them I would call one of them if I needed any help. I did not even want much assistance from Sal, either, because I felt a deep desire to focus inward. During the days, I saw him outside carrying around huge rocks for a wall that he was building. I smiled, knowing this was his way of laboring with me. I prayed to Mary through every contraction and experienced her as my labor support. Her presence was warm and supportive. She knew my grief, she knew my pain, and She gave me the strength to labor for three days without a break.

I monitored the progress of my labor and kept track of my blood loss and food and fluid intake. On the third day, after being in the most intense stage of labor for eight uninterrupted hours, I recognized that I was losing too much blood and was not able to think clearly anymore. I called Nancy, who lived right up the road, and asked her to please come quickly, for I thought I might be hemorrhaging. Sal had gone to bed, following my earlier suggestion. I had closed the door to the bedroom so my groans would not keep him awake. I really wanted to rely only on Mother Mary for my support. But now I began to think I had made a poor decision. Blood seemed to be gushing out of me. I called loudly for Sal, but he did not awaken. Nancy was not there yet, and I wondered whether I was going to die of blood loss. I imagined arriving before my Master Jesus and Mother Mary after passing through the transition of death and having to explain what I was doing there. I would have to admit that the cause of my death was plain stupidity, for which I would be very sorry. This thought was more disturbing to me than the intensity of the physical and emotional experiences I was having.

My mind was filled with these fears as I continued to yell for Sal and wondered what was taking Nancy so long. Though probably only a few minutes passed before Sal heard me and appeared, I had entered into an eternal zone, and he seemed to take forever. Sal helped me out of my pants and placed a bowl onto a chair, where I sat down. Now I could better evaluate what was happening, how much blood I was actually losing. As soon as I sat on the bowl, I felt the tiny body of our baby slip out of me. Instantly the bleeding stopped. "Oh, that bleeding was just the placenta releasing!" I said to Sal, my hindsight being 20/20. It all made sense now. At that moment Nancy came rushing in. I told her that the emergency was over; the bleeding had subsided.

Now I was stable, and after a bit Nancy returned home. Sal went back to bed after I told them both that I wanted to be alone again to take in all that had happened. I would sleep later. I picked up the little fetus. This was to have been my baby! How little it was. How sad to see this baby devoid of life. It was only about three and a half inches long. I examined it all over, now in my role as the midwife, looking for any clues as to why this baby had died. There was a tiny penis, so it was, in fact, a boy. The little body was perfect, except for being lifeless. The placenta and cord were also as they should be. I felt myself entering into a strange state of being in which I was at the portals of both birth and death. My heart and mind were experiencing both together, and I felt myself drawn into an awareness of standing at the gateway between the worlds. I could see figures of people passing by in both directions, moving from the unseen into incarnation on Earth, as well as from incarnation back into the spirit world. After holding the baby a bit, I went to Sal and showed it to him. Then I gently placed it in a bowl in the refrigerator and went to bed.

As I lay in bed, my altered state of consciousness increased. My awareness of the spiritual world became stronger and stronger. Then, quite suddenly, a being appeared right there in my bedroom. I was startled, though not really afraid. He was about eight feet tall, reaching all the way to the ceiling. He looked like he was in his 50s, a hefty kind of a guy, bald on the top. He wore a brown robe with a rope around his waist. He said to me, "Well it is about time you picked up! I have been trying to get through to you for three days." It was as if he was talking about calling me on the phone. He had an intense presence, like someone not to be messed with. He was not mean, but very strong and authoritative. I felt like I was seven years old as I sat there before him.

"Who are you?" I asked somewhat timidly.

He looked at me incredulously. "What do you mean? I was, of course, to be your baby!"

He said this as if I was indeed a bit dense and that what he said was the most obvious fact under the sun. I was stunned. *This* enormous character would have been *my* baby? My first thought was, "Oh my goodness, how would one potty-train someone of that intensity and determination!" Again I felt like I was seven years old. I could not imagine mothering—or worse yet, disciplining—this person.

"What is your name?" I asked him.

"Brother Alfonso," he replied. I cracked a smile. It struck me as humorous that, as my married last name was Cozzolino, he would have been Alfonso Cozzolino. It seemed a bit much.

"What is so funny?" he demanded. I told him my thoughts about the first and last name. He had no sense of humor on the matter at all. I quickly stifled my smile and decided to make use of this time to find out why this miscarriage had occurred.

I asked Brother Alfonso whether the miscarriage had been part of the plan all along, or was he actually going to be my baby. He said, "No, this was not part of the plan. I was going to be a part of your family."

"So why did this happen?" I asked.

"You needed a hole blown in your heart, and this seemed to be the best way to do that."

This was quite shocking news. "Why did I need that?" He told me that I had been actively destructive to the marriage and that I could not have the result of the union while I was seeking to destroy the union. He said I was now being held to a higher standard since I had dedicated myself to God and the path to God. This seemed to be an extreme result of my having been quarrelsome with Sal. I asked, "But why did God decide that I needed to be taught *this* particular way?"

Brother Alfonso answered (quoting Jesus), "Because 'where your treasure is, there will your heart be also.' We needed to get to your heart. Your treasure is in your children. So this loss was the means to get to your heart." I was appalled. This did not seem fair!

"But I did not know this rule, so why is God still holding me to it?"

"Ignorance of the law does not put you above the law," he answered.

It still felt wrong and as if the punishment did not fit the crime.

"But this feels harsh. That I would lose a baby over this?"

"Harsh?" he exclaimed. His voice was intense. "Harsh, you said? *This* is not harsh! You could have lost one of the children you already have."

I froze. Oh, my God, he was right. This was nothing in comparison to the thought of losing one of my existing kids. Then I *had* been let off easy! As I recovered from the shock of that thought, my attention returned to him. "So what about you? How does this affect you?"

"It is a setback," he said. "It is not easy to find good placements." I began to realize that he had just given up his life, at least in that body, and that he had done so as a gift to me.

"You gave your life just to teach me a lesson?" I asked in awe.

"To teach you a lesson?" He laughed. "No, not even that. I gave my life so that you *might* learn a lesson. It is to be seen whether you do!" I felt his eyes piercing me as he spoke. He did not seem too convinced that I necessarily would learn what I was meant to learn from this. "Besides," he said, "where I come from, people do that all the time—give their lives so that others *might* learn a lesson." He shrugged.

"Was Sal required to learn the same as my lesson?" I asked.

"No," he said. "This lesson was primarily for you. But he will also have the opportunity to learn from it." As I had had all my questions answered, Brother Alfonso took his leave of me and disappeared into the night.

I lay in bed pondering what had just transpired. I was definitely not sleeping, so Brother Alfonso's appearance was not a dream, and yet I had been carrying on this conversation without waking Sal, who was in bed next to me. I knew without a doubt that I had not imagined this encounter. What realm did it take place in? As I lay there, I noticed that I was still clearly at the portal of life and death. I could still perceive the souls passing in both directions, and I was filled with deep awe. I had been introduced to a person who functioned on a level of being where people regularly give up their lives so that someone *might* learn a lesson that *might* make a difference. After a long time, I fell asleep, amazed at the experiences of this day: the birth and death of one of my children, a near-death experience myself when I thought I was going to bleed to death, and then an encounter with a soul who would have been my son, had the pregnancy continued.

When I awoke in the morning, I was still in an altered state of consciousness. I was tired and sad at the loss but I also felt a heightened awareness of the spiritual world. I remained in that state for three days, during which I could still see the souls crossing over the portal of birth and death. I told people all around me what I was seeing. They were confounded by my words of life and death, and how I looked so full of peace and light, considering I had just had a second-trimester miscarriage. My friends, however, were respectful, even though they could not relate to what I was describing. They seemed to sense it was somehow holy, and they did not disturb me in my peaceful altered state.

When the children came back home the next day, I gave each of them individual time to show them the little baby, still attached to the small placenta by his umbilical cord. They all cried and grieved and expressed their loss. Nathan asked why none of his brothers stuck around, since first Ian and now this one had left. Sofia grieved at once again being the youngest, and Odessa and Pascale were sad to not have a baby to look forward to playing with. I did not tell the family of my encounter with Brother Alfonso. It felt too personal. Sal wanted to name the baby Gabriel, so I said his middle name was Alfonso. The children laughed at the name and asked why I chose it. I said: "It just *is* his name." That was all. I did not tell them the whole story until years later.

In the afternoon, we wrapped the tiny body and placenta in a white linen napkin and on it we placed a deep red rose from our garden. Sal dug a hole in the orchard behind our house, and with prayers and blessings, we buried Gabriel Alfonso there. The children recovered from their sadness over the next couple of months. Sal rarely mentioned it any more. For me, the experience remained one of the most remarkable events of my life. My consciousness about how I related to Sal increased dramatically. I resolved to try to be conscious to never again be destructive to our marriage.

One year later, on the anniversary of the birthday, I sat at my Mary Shrine and wept for the emptiness I felt in my arms that had no baby to hold. I looked up at the picture of Mother Mary, and the words that the prophet said to her after Jesus' birth came to mind: "And your heart also shall be pierced as with a sword." Ah, I thought, her heart was also broken over the loss of a son. Why? I then saw how it was through the piercing of our hearts that love can stream out. I saw that because my arms were empty, they could reach out to the entire world, which included Sal. Because I now knew of the great gifts and sacrifices others make for us without us often even knowing, I could open my heart and give freely. Though I learned to be aware of whether my actions, words, thoughts, and feelings were contributing to the growth or the demise of my marriage, through the piercing of my heart with the grief of losing this baby, I also learned to love other people with greater warmth and deeper compassion.

I remember Brother Alfonso often. I am ever so grateful to him for his gift and for what he taught me. When I was ordained a master teacher, I reached up to him and asked, "Did I learn the lesson? Was your sacrifice worth it?" I perceived his being connecting with mine and his approval and blessings coming my way. I can never think of that pregnancy and miscarriage as a loss. I can only think of them as blessings that I had the great good fortune of receiving. Brother Alfonso surely found another family to incarnate into, and must be a teenager now. I look forward to meeting him someday. I am sure I will recognize the power of that personality no matter what its form, male or female, large or small. Whatever body he is in, that light will shine through, and I will rejoice to get to know him.

9

SEEING THE FACE OF GOD: SELF-REALIZATION AS THE THIRD INITIATION OF THE INNER PATH

When Thou didst say, Seek ye my face; my heart said unto thee, Thy face, Lord, I will seek.

—Psalm 27:8

A Retreat and The Experience of Self-Realization

The following summer, the order held a four-day retreat in a beautiful rural location in southern Indiana. I had never met many of the members of the order who came from other states. Great excitement bubbled up all around for this opportunity to gather, give, and receive, and be raised up and deepened. Because I was mostly alone in my practices in Kentucky, I may have been the happiest one of all to have this time together with what I was beginning to feel were my brothers and sisters in this work and on this path to God. But I was not the only one feeling ecstatic about this immersion into spiritual intensity, inner growth, and loving relations with others. We all seemed to be of one heart and mind in our enthusiasm and dedication to our own spiritual growth and our service to others.

Each day began with meditation in the morning, followed by communion. The three master teachers and the priests took turns serving us. Morning communion was so powerful that I was blitzed by breakfast time. The days were filled with lectures, individual meetings with the teachers, and relaxing times with the other attendees. After the evening lecture, we had prayers and devotional singing together. This prayer and song time often became so moving and ecstatic as we all joined in expressing our love and devotion to God that I went off to bed as if to sleep in the arms of the angels.

On the second night, the teachers asked everyone except for me to stay out of the chapel until summoned. I tried to not speculate what was going to happen, and since I in fact did not have any idea, I remained calm, knowing that God was about to bless me in some way. Master Peter and another teacher named Master John posted a priest outside the door to prevent any intrusions. Over the next hour or so, these two master teachers did what only true master teachers are empowered to do: they removed the veil that covered the God-Self at the center of my being and brought me face to face with my creator. I was overwhelmed with awe and felt so humbled before my God that tears poured from my eyes. Now everything in heaven and on earth made sense. Now I understood for the first time who I was, who God was, and how all of life and the cosmos fit together. I saw creation laid out before me, and as the book of Genesis tells us that when God created the world He/She saw that it was all good, so I now also saw that all that was created was good.

After the initiation I could hardly stand, much less walk. The teachers helped me get back to a chair by the altar, where I sat in amazement at the glory and magnificence of God while the other people returned to the chapel and began to sing and pray. Tears of joy, gratitude, and awe continued to flow down my cheeks. A minister brought me bedding so I could sleep right there in the chapel near the altar, which was lit only by the Eternal Flame candle. Sleeping was difficult because the new awareness and expansion of my consciousness was so immense. Yet when I rose in the morning, I felt as if I would never need sleep again. I was fresh and so full of light, life, and love that I easily participated in another full day. I did take time to be alone in the next days, to let the immensity of the blessing sink in. Everything I had ever thought to be true and all the beliefs I had held about the world, others, and myself entered my mind for reconsideration in the light of what I now understood. God was showing me how God sees things, how God thinks and feels, how God relates to us. I never before had felt so much of God's love. I could tell that my soul also felt a great sense of relief. I felt it saying, "Thank God we made it back to Him/Her again!" It seemed like my soul had at times thought I was going to miss the boat completely during this life. I quite distinctly felt on a soul level that I had returned home after a long and precarious time away. I was home, in God, once again.

Blessings and Challenges For Those Who Have Been Self-Realized

Self-realization, or what is also referred to as God-realization, is once again an initiation, meaning a beginning, not a completion, of a level of being in relationship with God. Master teachers give it to those who, after receiving the initiation of illumination, have diligently worked with the light that has filled their bodies, minds, and hearts and who have gone much deeper in their love and desire for God. Through working with that light inside of them, they continue to increase its strength. By longing and reaching for God, they begin to create the channel that will allow them to approach God directly. Even with all these things accomplished, the aspirant to God will still need a master teacher who has been trained and empowered to perform this initiation, to rend the veil that covers the God-Self and open that great reality up for them. The teacher will not do this until their students have truly readied themselves and want God above all else.

More is never said about these initiations because to do so would be the greatest wrong one could ever do to another person. If a person told you what their experience was, you might then create concepts in you mind of what to expect. Later, if you yourself become ready to be brought into this reality, your concepts would likely get in the way of your having a true and real experience. Even if you did have a real experience, you would likely doubt it because you would wonder if you simply experienced what you expected to experience from what you had heard. Or, if your experience differed from that of the other person you heard it from, you would question whose was better and whose was more real. All these things could get in the way of your coming before the God of your soul with no expectations, being open to whatever way God wished to reveal God's Self to you.

This initiation is entirely unimaginable until you have experienced it for yourself. Then the changes brought about throughout your life will be limited only by your willingness to allow the changes. All of life will take on a new luster, a new truth, as you will then see life and understand it as God meant it to be. Because it is an initiation, a beginning, the spiritual aspirant will then need to take this gift and go ever deeper into it. The door to direct contact is open, but one must spend time every day getting to know God and conversing with God. It is now much easier to hear what might before have been aptly described as "the still, small voice" inside. But it takes discipline and care to not become complacent, thereby neglecting to nurture and develop this newfound relationship. Otherwise the clarity of the connection will dim, as would the connection with any human being if the relationship were not maintained and developed.

When a soul has attained to certain knowledge of God and has made connections with beings in the spiritual world, the knowledge is not lost when the person leaves that incarnation. It remains on the soul, and often a soul, upon reincarnating, will still have some of the knowing they have already attained available to them. Yet, each soul must, in each incarnation, decide once again whom they will serve. Will they pursue the things of Earth or the things of heaven during this particular lifetime?

Even for those who in a previous life were highly accomplished in their spiritual development, there is a significant danger that they will not find their way back to God in a subsequent incarnation. Or, after finding their way back to God, they might fall down on their commitment to serve God and thereby return to a condition of incurred negative karma. Therefore each soul who asks to come back to Earth once they are free from having to return is making a significant sacrifice, as they might well end up in worse karmic condition at the end of each life than they were at the beginning. Many souls are incarnated at this time who were previously saints and teachers and yet have not managed to live up to their eternal vows in this life. It is never easy, and yet the choice is always ours to make. If we have the humility, the desire, and the will to serve in accordance with our commitments and our mission, God will always provide the way. However, we will have to choose God above all else: above our families of origin, above our spouses, above our children, above our pride, and above our wanting of all kinds for ourselves. God alone; that is the way Jesus taught, and He meant it.

In Matthew 5:8, Jesus said, "Blessed are the pure in heart, for they shall see God." How can we go about becoming pure in heart? How did we lose the purity of our hearts in the first place? Over our many lifetimes we have had many painful experiences. As a result of these experiences, we have developed anger and numerous fears and resentments. Sometimes along with those feelings, we also developed significant amounts of jealousy, aggression, and hatred. Trust is often the first casualty of painful experiences, and it is the last wound to heal. Without it, we cannot enter into any relationships of depth or meaning, including relationships with ourselves, with a spiritual teacher, and with God.

In order to see God we will need to heal all the wounds and the results of those wounds. We can no longer carry fears, resentments, anger, jealousy, aggression, or hatred. Every one of those is lodged in our hearts until we bring it to light, confess it, and allow it to be lifted from us. We have to forgive and be forgiven. We have to trust and become trustworthy to people around us and to God.

All this is part of the purification of the heart. Only through allowing ourselves to be brought through this process and actively working to clear all such darkness from our hearts will we come to be able to actually see God, face to face.

The Four-Year Old Daughter Who Saw and Spoke With Angels

My middle daughter, Pascale, was four years old when she learned what the word "angel" meant. We had no books on the subject in the house. She did not attend school, nor did she spend time in other households, for we were quite isolated in our country homestead. She seems to have been seeing beings that were not in physical bodies all her life. She had not known what to call them until she figured out that the word "angel" must refer to what she saw. She began talking about them quite casually, assuming everyone saw them as she did. Once when we were talking, she asked, "Mommy, why are there so many different kinds of angels?"

"What kinds of angels do you see?"

"Oh, all kinds. There are the tall thin ones whose feet you can't see. There are the ones that look like cute little babies. And we all have our own, too." She mentioned angels that play music, as well as some others. She spoke of them just as they are described in books on angels that tell us what different forms and functions angels can have. And yet, I knew for a fact that she had never seen such a book. I was amazed, and still somewhat skeptical, yet I could not come up with any explanation for what Pascale said, except that she, in fact, saw angels, frequently and everywhere.

One day at the dinner table Pascale said, "I wonder why all of our own angels are different sizes?"

Nathan jumped right into verbally harassing her, as he usually did when she spoke of angels. "You do not see angels! You are lying or just imagining it!"

Pascale began to cry. "I *do* see them! I *do*!"

I corrected Nathan, as I always did when this happened, telling him that no one can know what another person does or does not see. One can only say what one sees oneself. Nathan begrudgingly stopped and slowly settled down. When everyone at the table was once again calm, I asked Pascale, "So, are all our angels different sizes?"

She happily chirped, "Oh, yes! Pa's is the biggest. Nathan's is the next biggest. Then there's Odessa's, Sofia's, and then mine. And yours, Mommy, is the smallest." I was at a loss for an explanation for her. Besides, by now I had learned that she tended to find her own answers if I simply left her alone. Pascale furrowed her little brow as she was thinking about how this came to be. Soon her face lit up and she proclaimed, "I know why Pa's is the biggest! It is because he needs the *most* help!"

Sal had his mouth wide open; he was about to put a forkful of pasta in it. He froze mid-bite at this declaration that he was in the greatest need of help. Sal at least somewhat knew Pascale was right. He did not have a spiritual practice. He only read books about Sufism, but rarely did any of the practices he had learned in the Sufi school. He knew he had lost control over cigarettes and indulged in various other earthly temptations. His anger often got the better of him, and he could be moody for weeks on end. So yes, he did not dispute that he needed the most help.

Pascale went right on, oblivious of the consternation she was causing. "And Nathan needs the *next* most help; and then Odessa, then Sofia, and then me. Hmmm, I wonder why Mommy's is the smallest? Oh, I know! It is because Mommy is already learning to talk to God!" Her expression changed into one of satisfaction at having solved the mystery. Nathan, however, could not hold his tongue anymore and, in spite of my attempts at swift intervention, he began to taunt her until her tears ran again. Our own little cherub wasn't feeling very appreciated. To Sal's credit, he never indicated that he did not believe her, and he did not even defend himself against the charge that he needed the most help. He simply accepted the "truth from the mouths of babes" and continued eating his pasta.

One night I sent Pascale up to bed in the loft that was the girls' bedroom. She had been there only a minute when she called down. "Mommy, I can't get into my bed."

"Why?" I called back to her.

"Because there are too many angels in it."

"Tell them that you have to go to bed, and ask them to move over," I said.

A moment later Pascale's voice came back from the loft. "Okay, they moved over. Good-night!"

Another time Pascale posed the question, "Why does Nathan's angel ask me almost every night where Nathan's room is?"

I answered, "I don't know, Pascale. Why does he?"

Pascale pondered this one a bit and then said, "Oh, I think it is because he is spacey. Nathan is spacey, so his angel is spacey, too." That seemed to satisfy her question. She trotted off. Four-year old Pascale often told me how, when she went to bed at night, she could see God and Mother Mary right there through the ceiling above her bed.

One day I asked her, "Pascale, what does God look like?"

She looked surprised. "Don't you know?" she asked.

"Yes, but I wondered what God looks like to you." She seemed at a loss for words to describe God. So I asked, "Is God an old man with a beard?"

She burst out laughing. "Why, Momma? Is that what people think?"

"Some people do," I replied.

She found that quite amusing. She thought again how to describe what God looked like. Finally she said, "I don't know how to describe God, because there is so much light I can't make out God's form." I was amazed at the clarity of Pascale's experience of God and I never again asked her about what she saw.

One day, when Pascale was four, she came into the kitchen and said to me, "Mommy, it is time that I teach you about God."

I looked at her half amused, half curious, and asked, "You want to teach me about God?"

She said, "Yes. Put me up on the counter so I can teach you." Not sure how I was to respond to this, but certainly with some air of amusement, I sat her on the kitchen counter, where she was now eye to eye with me (which seemed to be her intention). She then said, "To get to know God you need to do three things: You need to think about God a lot, so God's thinking becomes your thinking. You need to love God a lot, so that God's heart becomes your heart. And you need to start acting like God, so that God's life becomes your life."

I was speechless. I pondered what she had just said to me and tried to fathom what it meant and how one would apply it. She was just watching me, not cracking the least bit of a smile. She then said, "Okay, that is enough for today. Put me down." Now I was obedient without any air of amusement in my response. I put her down and she went off, a regular four-year-old back at play. I stood in the kitchen trying to comprehend what had just happened. My four-year-old daughter had imparted to me a teaching about drawing close to God that was more profound than what most adults would ever aspire to understand in a lifetime. How did she know that? Obviously she had not obtained such knowledge in this life. She had never been anyplace where she might have heard such things. As I had never heard this particular teaching myself, she certainly had not learned it from me.

A couple of weeks later, she came to me again in the kitchen and asked to be put on the counter so she could teach me more about God. This time I did it with respect and happiness that more teachings were coming my way. Once again I was told one or two profound sentences, after which she asked me to put her down again, and she returned to her play. The sessions took place every week or two and totaled approximately six or seven lessons. I gave Pascale complete freedom regarding these interactions. I did not bring them up for discussion, but only listened while she taught.

I asked Master Peter how I should respond to Pascale's angel sightings and to her teaching me about God. He told me to simply validate what she saw and knew and to be supportive. He predicted that her sight would probably go away once she was about seven years old, when the age of reason began. He said that is usually the pattern. Many children see beings and things from the world that is otherwise thought of as invisible. Usually their parents shut that down in them by telling them that what they see is imaginary. Pascale still had an open channel to what she had learned and knew from her previous lifetimes. When she came to depend on reason more, she would most likely close off that channel.

Master Peter turned out to be right. When Pascale was seven years old, she spoke less and less of seeing angels. By the time she was 10, she no longer saw anything otherworldly and began to question the entire experience. I was glad that Master Peter had foretold this so I was not shocked or surprised by it. When she was 12, she asked to speak with me privately one day. As we sat together, she told me that she had to tell me the truth. She said that she was now convinced that she had made up all the stories of visions and knowing about God, and she felt very guilty that she had deceived me that way. I hugged her and told her that I knew for a fact that she had *not* made it all up because there was no way she could have known what she knew. I told her the details of angels that she had reported seeing and the knowledge about God that she had expressed could only have been available to her from her own experience. I reassured her that it was normal for her to no longer see those things, and it was also normal for her to now doubt the reality of the experiences themselves. I said, "You did not have to work for your eyes remaining open to the heaven world as a young child, because you had already attained it in a previous life. But now your eyes are closed to all that glory and that truth. If you choose to reestablish contact with that world as an adult, you will have to work for it and make the sacrifices necessary to have that once again."

When Pascale was 19 years old, she came to me on this matter once again. Weeping, she said, "Now I know why I chose you as my mother. During those years that I could not hold the truth of what I saw and knew, you held it for me. Now I am ready to do as you said and to begin to make my way back to that connection with God and the heaven world. Thank you so much for believing in what I had experienced even when I could not. Now I know it was true, and I want to find it again."

Pascale chose to begin training with the Order of Christ/Sophia shortly thereafter, entirely of her own accord. She did not choose this because I was a co-director of the Order. In fact, she would have preferred that she could enter as everyone else does. She was given no privileges beyond what other students are given. I was never her teacher, as we do not want family members to be teaching each other. Master Peter taught her, and she was not spared any rigor in her training. Pascale was ordained a priest in that Order at the age of 23, having reestablished her connections and visions of God and that world that is usually deemed "unseen."

The Five-Year Old Son Who Was Tormented With a Past-Life Memory

Sometimes a memory from a past life can be so awful that a soul cannot manage to live *this* life until it is healed. Such was the case with my son Nathan. Our family had recently moved to the farm in Kentucky. We were still living in a school bus that had been converted into a camper. Odessa was eight, Nathan was five, and Pascale was two when Nathan began to have a recurring nightmare. He could not remember what it was about when he awoke, but he fell out of bed whenever he had it. He was sleeping on the top bunk, and Sal was sleeping below him. When he began to stir and make the noises that indicated he was having the nightmare again, Sal would stick his arm out, ready to catch Nathan when, a moment later, he predictably came falling out of his bed. Each time, Sal pulled him into bed with him and they both went back to sleep. After six months of building, we finally could move out of the school bus/camper and into our very unfinished house. Nathan continued to have the dream frequently. We did not think too much of it, since he really could not remember anything when he woke.

Within the year, however, Nathan's problem seemed to be deepening. Now he actually got up out of bed and sleepwalked. His bedroom was directly above ours, and each night when I heard his feet hit the floor, I headed for the steps and reached him just as he was coming down. He seemed to be heading for the front door. He was quite frightened and felt the need to run away, but by the time I got him awake he looked at me blankly, having no idea how he got to where he was or what he might have been dreaming. Each night I took him back to bed. In the morning he was oblivious to anything having ever happened. None of my other children sleepwalked, but I continued to hope that he was simply going through some stage that he would soon outgrow.

The next spring, Nathan began behaving very strangely during the day, too. The first time I noticed something was seriously wrong was when I had him with me in a store and I went around the end of an aisle, out of his sight. When he looked up and could not see me, instead of looking for me in the next aisle, he ran for the door of the store, out into the parking lot, and down the street. Fortunately, I saw him as he headed out the door. I ran after him, calling his name, but he did not seem to hear me. I caught up with him as he was hightailing down a main street as if the devil was chasing him. When I caught him, stopped him, and made him look at me, he seemed at first to be in a daze. Then he shook himself out of it and could not give me much information about what he was doing. He only said that he didn't see me and thought I was gone.

Nathan's odd behavior increased in frequency. When we took him shopping, we had to make sure he could always see us. Generally, when we were out, we held his hand. His behavior seemed so strange, as this was a child who had never before been afraid of being away from us and had stayed happily with babysitters. He could never tell us much about what possessed him to act as he did. Our concern was growing.

Whenever we left the farm to go out, on our way back home, we had to drive a mile down a rock road beyond the last paved street of our tiny country town. The last stretch of this rock road consisted of a very steep hill, after which one had to drive across a creek that had no bridge. When it rained the creek rose, and sometimes we had to leave our Jeep on the side of the creek and climb across on two logs that were felled across it about a hundred yards up-creek.

This particular day, I took Odessa shopping with me. Sal, Nathan, and Pascale stayed home. The rain fell heavily all day, so when I reached the creek, I left the Jeep and went to assess how deep the water was and whether we should risk driving across. The water was pretty deep and the current seemed strong, but I didn't want to have to climb across the logs with all the groceries. I hiked up my dress and waded in to test the depth and strength of the flow. The water came up to my thighs. I could not get even halfway across before the current nearly washed my legs out from under me. I knew the Jeep would not make it across. Odessa and I picked up the bags of groceries and made our way upstream along the creek to the crossing logs.

Meantime, Sal looked out the window and saw us heading to the crossing place. He told Nathan to keep an eye on Pascale while he came out to help Odessa and I get the groceries across the creek. I was eight months pregnant with Sofia and was not so fond of trying to balance on the logs while carrying the bags. I welcomed Sal's appearance when he came to help us. The entire process of carrying the bags up our side of the creek, climbing across, and getting back into the house could not have taken more than five to eight minutes. When we reached the house, however, Pascale was crying, and Nathan was nowhere to be seen. Sal and I ran out of the house calling for him. He seemed to have vanished. A steep hill rose behind our house, and in front of it was the raging creek. Sal went downstream along the creek and I headed upstream. As we ran, we called out his name. When I had gone as far as I could imagine that Nathan might have wandered upstream, I ran, holding my very pregnant belly, back downstream to see if Sal had found him. Sal was just returning from downstream. He looked shaken, as if he could not believe what was happening. I cried out to him, "Why did you come back without Nathan?"

He said, "I went to the point where the creek joins another creek. The two become a raging river. If Nathan tried to cross there, or fell in and washed beyond that place…" The conclusion was too horrible to utter. At this point, I went wild with fear and grief. Sal tried to calm me but I was beside myself.

I walked aimlessly in circles in the grass, crying out in despair. Nathan must have tried to cross the creek but was washed away and drowned. We would probably never even find his body! Here I was about to give birth to a baby, and I had just lost my son. It was too unbearable to even get my mind around it. Though Sal tried to console me, I continued walking in circles, weeping out loud. "He's gone! He's gone! My Nathan is gone!" I fell in a huddle on the grass, stricken with grief and horror.

As I sat there I heard Nancy's voice coming from the top of the hill on the other side of the creek. I looked up and could not believe my eyes: Beside Nancy stood Nathan, holding her hand. As she and Nathan came down the hill, Sal and I watched them, dumbfounded, trying to recover our senses. Sal kept saying, "Oh thank God, oh thank God! Nathan is alive!" I could not speak at all. It seemed like a mirage. How did he get across the creek? We had been on the crossing logs, so he could not have crossed there. Sal and I swooped Nathan up in our arms and wept with relief. He was a bit worried that he was in big trouble. We just held him. Once inside the house, we waited until we were all sitting and had somewhat calmed down. Then we asked, "Nathan, how did you get across the creek?"

He seemed surprised by our question. He said, "I walked across."

"Where?" we asked him. "Where did you walk across?"

"At the road, where we always cross."

"No, Nathan," I said. "That is not possible."

"But I did," he insisted. "It wasn't hard at all. Look, I didn't even get water in my boots." He reached down and pulled off his little red boots and showed us the insides. One by one we each took the boot and examined it. And one by one we dropped into a stunned silence. The inside of the boot was completely dry!

There could be no doubt that Nathan crossed the creek, because he had, in fact, come back from the other side. There was no doubt he did not cross on the logs, as we crossed there. He seemed to have gone across water that was at least two-and-a half feet deep without getting water inside his five-inch-tall boots. And he said he did it without any effort at all! There was only one explanation: We were in the presence of a miracle. I had images of Nathan's guardian angel grabbing him by the nape of his neck and carrying him across the water. Or somehow Nathan walked *on* the water, with the help of a beneficent spirit of God. Little Nathan still looked worried that he was in trouble, especially given the big deal we all seemed to be making about him crossing the creek. We took turns holding him close and thanking God for saving our son from what seemed like certain death.

We tried to keep an ever-closer eye on Nathan. One month later, I gave birth to Sofia there in our new house, with Sal, Odessa, Nathan, and Pascale around me. The day following Sofia's birth, Sal took Nathan and Pascale with him to pick something up at a friend's house. He told them to wait in the truck while he ran in. He came out a few minutes later and found Pascale crying and Nathan gone. Sal could not understand what had happened. Why did Nathan not come to the house if he was looking for Sal? Sal and his friend combed the area on foot and then began to drive the streets looking for Nathan. They stopped and informed the local police, and within the hour, only half a day after giving birth, I found myself hosting the headquarters of a search party for Nathan. All the available neighbors came out to help. Nathan was found an hour or two later, walking as fast as he could down a street with his customary look for such occasions, which was dazed and very frightened.

Something had to be done. Nathan was now endangering his life over and over again. I was sure that Nathan's recurring dream had to be related to what happened to him during the day. I initiated an intense effort to find out what the dream was. I talked with Nathan before he went to sleep and told him that he had to tell himself to remember what he was dreaming when he awoke. When I met him at the stairs sleepwalking, I called to him and gently shook him to wake him up so he could tell me the dream. Finally, over some weeks' time, the details of the nightmare emerged.

Nathan said that he was older in the dream. When I asked him how old, he said he was the same age as a boy we knew who was 16. He described himself as being at the bottom of what must have been a kind of well. The walls were round and brick, and there was a bit of water in the bottom. He said that his father and another man were standing at the top of the well talking. I asked Nathan whether his father was Sal. He looked befuddled, and said, "No, it was a different father." He said he was there waiting for his father to get him out. The two men went away after a while. Nathan got colder and colder and hungry and thirsty, too. He waited and waited. He could not understand why his father did not return. I asked him where his mother was. He said that she was several fields away from there, at their home. I asked whether I was his mother. He once again looked baffled and said, "No, it was another mother." I asked whether his mother knew he was down there. He said he did not think so.

Nathan could not tell me how long he was in the well, but he said it was very long. I asked him how he got out. He looked even more confused and bothered and said, "I didn't!" Then he burst into tears. "Why did my father not come back? He knew I was there! How could he just leave me there?" Nathan's little body shook in grief and fear as he remembered the feelings of the dream. His mind seemed to short out when he tried to comprehend why his father had left him there to die. How could a father do that? He hadn't done anything wrong. "Why? Why? Why?" he cried. I held him as he shook, and reminded him that we *were* with him, and we would never abandon him like that. I told him we loved him, and we were *not* those people, so he was now safe with us.

We had hoped that Nathan would be helped by recalling the dream and by us reassuring him that we were not those parents and would never leave him. But it did not. Nathan was getting more lost in that world as the days passed, and we knew something had to be done immediately. We did not want to take him to psychiatrists because we knew they were quite unlikely to identify this, as we did, as a past-life trauma. They would declare that Nathan was psychotic, that he was losing touch with reality, and he would at the very least be medicated—possibly institutionalized. In our view, this would traumatize the poor kid even more and would not address the problem at all. I called Master Peter and asked for his help. Master Peter said that what Nathan needed was a memory healing, and since he, my teacher, was not with us, I would have to do it myself. He explained in detail what I needed to do and expressed confidence in my ability to help Nathan heal.

Nathan hated talking about the dream. He became upset any time he thought about it. This child who had once been a happy and carefree boy was now fearful and seemingly psychotic. He was six years old, very bright, and quite disturbed. I told him that he was going to have to think and talk about the dream one more time for me to be able to help him. He said, "No, Momma, I don't want to think about it! I hate it!" I held him and told him that we were going to ask God to take it away from him for good, but that he would first have to enter back into the memory of it. I finally persuaded him. I incensed the house to prepare the space for the healing. I brought Nathan into our little chapel and set him on a chair right in front of the altar. I stood behind him with my hands on his shoulders and asked for the presence of Jesus and Mary to come and be with us. As I felt their presence fill the room, I asked that they take over this healing and direct it so that Nathan could be whole and go on with his life.

I told Nathan to imagine himself back in the well. I assured him that I was staying right there with him and would keep my hands on his shoulders to support him. I asked him to close his eyes and tell me what he saw. He once again described the horror of his father abandoning him in the well. He described experiencing his time in the well as interminably long. I silently prayed that Jesus and Mary come save him from this memory, change it into something he could live with, and thereby heal him. I was saying nothing to Nathan, except urging him to stay there in the vision and see what happened. As he described getting so cold that he could no longer move, when he must have been near death, he suddenly said that something different was happening. He said, "Look! Look! Jesus has come! He has come to me! He is picking me up and taking me out of here. He came to get me!" He then described how Jesus picked him up, held him, and carried him up and away from there. Nathan was very animated when describing this part. "It feels *so* good with Jesus holding me!" Nathan's voice and expression changed completely. I could see how happy he was relaxing in Jesus' arms as he was taken away from the horrid well.

Now safe, Nathan asked Jesus, "Why did my father leave me there?"

Jesus said, "It doesn't matter now. Your father was very wrong to leave you. You are now safe." Nathan could accept that, and as my hands were still on his shoulders, I felt his whole body relax under my touch. I put my hands on his head and called down a blessing on him that the healing be complete and permanent. I thanked Jesus so much for saving Nathan from the well and from his terrible aloneness and fear. Nathan continued to feel Jesus' closeness and walked out of the chapel with a smile on his face.

Nathan slept through the night for the first time in over a year. He never again had the dream. His behavior returned to normal, and he was no longer worried when he didn't see us for a moment. In a very short time, he hardly remembered that he had ever had the bad dream. Within a year or so, he had no memory of it ever happening. I never brought it up to him until he was 18 years old. At that time I told him the whole story. I thought he should know because it is part of his history. I explained that I had not wanted to tell him before because that memory had been healed and replaced by a new one, and I did not want to reawaken the old one again. At 18 he had a very distant memory of having had some issue that was difficult, but had no recollection of what it pertained to. He was whole, and we felt immensely grateful.

As this story about Nathan illustrates, a person can sometimes be so tormented by a past-life trauma that they cannot function in this life. Nathan's father of that life nearly killed him again in this lifetime, through the trauma he had inflicted on him in the previous life. When people do not recognize the truth that souls reincarnate, they may miss a vital piece of information regarding what is tormenting a person. Nathan would have received intense medication and possible institutionalization at the hands of psychiatrists. His actual needs could only be addressed by knowing that the problem lay in his last life and could be healed through a spiritual process. I felt as though Nathan may have chosen me to be his mother because he knew he was going to need someone who would be able to identify and heal the problem. I was glad to be able to help him. The trauma he endured in his last life was bad enough without him losing this life over it. What would he have done in his next incarnation? Suffered again, until in some life he found someone who could help him? What a tragedy that would have been!

Without knowing of the existence of the soul and of its eternal life, during which it takes on many bodies on earth, we miss out on much of what is needed to understand human beings. Years later when I became a psychotherapist, I often shook my head in dismay at how this profession thinks it can help people heal though it does not even know that we are souls with long past histories. I was equally appalled that this profession frowns upon psychotherapists acknowledging and working with the spiritual world. I did not heal Nathan. I set the stage and asked for Jesus and/or Mary to heal him. Jesus did this in response to my request, as he taught: "Ask, and you shall receive." Alone, I could never have done what he did. Psychotherapy, by not acknowledging and relating to the spiritual world, cuts itself off from the greatest source of healing.

Souls can and do get deeply hurt. Souls need to find healing in order to be able to become pure in heart and to find and see God at the center of their beings. No one can approach God within them and receive the initiation of Self-realization if they have not healed to the point where they can trust completely. They have to be able to trust their teacher and trust God without reservation. I give great thanks for those who have handed us down the knowledge of how to heal the wounds of hearts and souls and have thereby brought us the possibility of meeting and coming to know God through direct experience. Due to the perseverance of teachers throughout the ages, all people who find a real teacher, who commit and give themselves completely over to healing and loving, can come through mystical baptism into illumination and, if they persist on their journey, can eventually enter into this, the third initiation of the Inner Path.

10

THE CALL TO SERVICE: TRAINING, MINISTERING, AND A TEACHER WHO FAILED

Until one is committed there is hesitancy, the chance to draw back, always ineffectiveness. Concerning all acts of initiative (and creation), there is one elementary truth, the ignorance of which kills countless ideas and splendid plans: that the moment one definitely commits oneself, then Providence moves, too. All sorts of things occur to help one that would never otherwise have occurred. A whole stream of events issues from the decision, raising in one's favor all manner of unforeseen incidents and meetings and material assistance, which no man could have dreamt would come his way. I have learned a deep respect for one of Goethe's couplets: 'Whatever you can do, or dream you can, begin it. Boldness has genius, power, and magic in it.'

—W.H. Murray, *The Scottish Himalayan Expedition*, 1951

The Failure and Loss of the Teacher

My astonishment and amazement at the wonders of the spiritual path and working with a teacher grew each day. Wouldn't everybody want to do this if they only knew about it? Master Peter smiled at my unbridled enthusiasm. He explained to me that many people are uninterested in the spiritual path, often because they do not know what it can do for them. Some are simply too caught up in daily life to even consider God.

"But can't we do more to let those who *are* interested know that this exists?"

Master Peter told me there were billions of people on the planet, but only a few who knew the path and had been trained to teach it.

"Are you trying to tell me that you want to help?" he asked.

"Yes! Yes! And yes again!" I could hardly contain myself.

"Okay," he said. "I will ask for inner guidance, and if I am told to, I will start training you to be a servant of God. Do you feel ready to begin training for the ministry?"

Most people begin the path motivated by a wish to grow and to experience less pain and separation from God, from oneself, and from others. The desire to teach or serve as a minister often does not come up until later, when the joy and gratitude for what you have received rises up and fills your heart with the desire to bring this healing to others. When that occurs in our school and the student tells his or her priest or teacher, the teacher then asks for guidance on beginning the training. God determines if this person is to be trained, and if so, when to begin. Students may be called to the ministry, or they may be called to give themselves in service in a different way. Our order also has opportunities for students to become Life-Vowed Brothers or Sisters, who commit to be of service in a particular way to the Order. Their vows, as binding as those taken by a minister, are lifelong. The difference is that they don't teach, minister, or work with the sacraments.

Though I was exuberant at the prospect of getting more training and of being a part of the great brother/sisterhood of those who pass on the mysteries of the inner path to others, I was also somewhat embarrassed by the thought of having to identify myself publicly as a Christian. I had some worries about having to talk to others about Jesus and Mary. None of my friends were Christian. I could easily have brought up any other kind of spirituality with them, but Christian spirituality? I was going to be stretching them to get them to even consider it. Still, I felt my soul jumping with joy. I knew that the part of me that was hesitant was a smaller, more squeamish, worried-about-what-people-would-think part, and I did not want to give that small "me" any life. So I went with my soul's pull. Deep inside, I knew I could not only receive these teachings for me, but I *had* to bring them to others. Nothing in life could possibly be as important or blessed as to help heal the brokenhearted and reunite them with God within them. When Master Peter told me that the guidance he received confirmed my readiness for training, I was overwhelmed with joy.

I did feel that I had a calling. But what is a calling? I asked myself. Where does it come from? I had heard people talking about having callings. I wondered what they meant by that, and how they determined whether it was real. When I asked

Master Peter these questions, he explained to me that a true calling comes from the level of our souls and the God-Self within us. It is quite specific. It is the soul calling out to the mind and heart reminding them that we came into a body for this incarnation with a purpose, a mission. When we hear that call, we know that we have to do this particular thing or we will have wasted our lives. A calling to serve by bringing the spiritual path to others comes from an even deeper place. It comes from God. Only God can draw others to God and ask them to be a part of God's own work of bringing souls back to their divine source. "How can I know if I have such a calling?" I asked.

"You might not know for a while," Master Peter said. "You might be put off by all the manifestations of such service that you have seen around you. When you experience the power and the healing of God's gifts coming through that channel yourself, your heart flames up in a desire to bring this healing and peace to others who are still in pain. And the more you let yourself yield to the thought of serving in this way, the clearer your life seems and the more a feeling of elation rises up in your soul."

Master Peter went on to explain how God needs people on earth who are willing to be changed into conscious men and women to work alongside those unseen beings who labor unwaveringly for the transformation of the Earth and its people. God does not need people who are already perfect. God only needs them to let God form them through the teacher He sends them. God needs them to be humble enough to take instruction, loving enough to care more about others than about their own self-centered needs, and trusting enough to accept that God will protect and care for them. If they will agree to give themselves over to God, God can make them a part of the divine brother/sisterhood of God's servants.

I began to understand that I could hope for no greater joy than to find that I have a calling and to have an opportunity to respond to it and embrace it. I felt much more like I was being given an opportunity to receive even more blessing than that I was taking on an obligation to help others. As St. Francis of Assisi said, "For it is in giving that we shall receive." In fact, there is no greater blessing than to be able to bless others. As that truth sank in, I knew I would never need to fear giving and serving. I knew I would learn to give up my self-centeredness and simply ask how I could help. I sensed that with that act alone, most of my life's problems would fall away, effortlessly.

In the order that Master Peter was directing, the first rung on the ladder of service was to become an ordained minister/deacon. My training consisted of a thorough study of the New Testament, of the books from which we teach our Tree of Life classes, and of various other books and writings. Deacons in these orders are also authorized to preside over Sunday services in the absence of a priest, and to give communion, though it is of a different format than the communion the priests serve. Deacons can teach classes and baptize adults and children. I had much to learn to prepare to offer all these services.

The training for working with the sacraments was astonishingly powerful. The first time I went to the altar and said the words of the ministers' communion while holding up the paten and the chalice, I was nearly bowled over by the energy that came down on the sacred vessels and on me. I had experienced the descent of great power during my initiations, but here it was descending for a sacrament that was performed daily! Was I to be given the opportunity to enter into such states every day?

Because I lived so far away, I was once again in the situation of not being able to be present for as much training as I would have wanted. Whenever I was there, Master Peter gave me intensive instruction, and he continued to teach me at least once a week through long phone conversations. Because this is a mystical path, much of what needs to occur in a student before he or she can be ordained a deacon does not take place as a result of learning the various duties or studying the texts. Instead, the student needs to be transformed. This takes a different amount of time for each person, and sometimes it turns out after a student begins training that he or she is actually not willing to be changed. The fact that one is allowed to begin training for ministry does not guarantee when, or even if, one will be ordained.

When the priest or master teacher training the student sees that the trainee is moving through transformation, they ask the Self within whether that student is ready for ordination. Only when the inner guidance directs it is a student ordained. My ordination as a minister-deacon brought up in me a feeling of connection to many past lifetimes, and I felt as if I was finally opening the door to my purpose for being on Earth. Though Sal had concerns and often resisted my activities that related to the Order, he agreed to build a small chapel-room in my house, showing some support, at least, for what I was doing. Right away, I began teaching classes and holding Sunday services. I got over my embarrassment about being a Christian and convinced a number of my friends and acquaintances to join me for classes and services. Despite the fact that my training was less thorough than I would have liked, my enthusiasm and love for this way of life carried me beyond all other considerations. Over the next 15 months, I introduced 12 adults to these teachings and baptized them. I also baptized a similar number of children. I was on fire, and it was contagious.

Sal loved our farm. One day he showed me where on our land he wanted to be buried—obviously intending to stay living on our little farm the rest of his life. Very shortly after that, Mother Mary told me in meditation that She wanted us to move.

"How in the world am I supposed to convince Sal of that?" I asked her.

She answered: "Don't say anything to him. I will convince him."

I truly did have faith in Mother Mary, but it seemed unimaginable that Sal would change his mind about staying on the farm. I obediently kept my mouth shut and waited. Within 10 days of Mother Mary speaking to me, we were having dinner when Sal said, "You know, I have been thinking that it might be better for the children to be where there is more culture. I think we should consider moving to a major city."

I was completely dumbfounded. "Mother Mary, you are *really* good!" I said silently.

Master Peter had told me that I needed to be near a master teacher to get training to become a priest, which would be the next step for me along my path of service. He himself was moving to Milwaukee, and my only other option to live near a teacher would be near where Master John lived, which was in Springfield, Massachusetts. I started worrying how I would get Sal to move to one of those two unlikely places. Once again, Mother Mary told me to let Her do it. Sal then announced that he thought that perhaps we should check out Toronto, Canada. He said he had always wanted to go there and had heard it was a very beautiful city. I was shocked. How would I continue my training from there? Mother Mary told me once again to go along while she took care of everything. Sal and I went to Toronto for a long weekend. We did like the city, but we discovered that it would be hard to get a work permit. When we mulled this over, along with other difficulties pertaining to moving to Canada, Sal said, "You know, this city reminds me of Boston. I love the European feeling of Boston. Maybe we should move there."

I could not believe my ears. Boston was only an hour and a half away from Springfield, where the other teacher, Master John, lived. How did Mother Mary get Sal to think that way? I felt I had witnessed a first-class miracle. Within three months, we put our farm on the market, packed up a moving truck, and went to Boston. I had to reconsider everything I had previously thought about how to make things happen and get things done. I doubt I could have ever convinced Sal to move to Massachusetts, and yet Mother Mary did it in next to no time. This was a great lesson for me, and one for which I will always be grateful. In Boston, we bought a house in a low-income black neighborhood because we could not afford to buy one anywhere else, and we did not care what color the neighbors were. It turned out that one of the biggest gangs in town lived a half a block from us, which provided an education for the whole family.

I got a job as deputy director of a social service agency near where we lived. I was responsible for creating new programs for the fiscally underprivileged, a.k.a. the poor. My job entailed deciding what kind of programs the area needed and then creating them. I learned how to write grant proposals and started programs that taught parents how to discipline their children. I worked on getting job contracts for folks from the inner city in the new highway construction project, and at the same time I revamped the surplus food giveaway projects. Finally, I contracted to have a building built in which I founded and ran a transition house for homeless women with children. I learned an immense amount through this experience. As we had no money to hire staff for the house, I was the only staff during the first year. I selected the families that came into the house; I created the support programs for them, appointed a board of directors, worked out all the funding, and then coordinated the services for each mother and her children. In three years, I had created a program that became a model for other such projects in the Boston area. I was also completely burned out. I had learned more, hoped more, and been more disappointed than I had ever dreamed I could be in a job. I discovered how few of the chronically poor ever change, no matter how much help they get. After five years of living in the inner city and working with its population, I had had enough. I could no longer see the poor with the eyes of innocence that I'd had when I first began working with them. Instead I saw how stubbornly stuck most of them were, with no interest or motivation to do the work that would be needed to be responsible for providing for themselves. We packed up the family and moved to an outlying town where, for the first time, we experienced suburban life. We had now lived in a nice city neighborhood in Louisville, a farm in rural Kentucky, and the deep inner city of Boston. I felt that I was becoming well rounded through my experiences of living in different environments. In future years, this knowledge would be helpful when students from all walks of life came to me to for instruction. My firsthand experiences allowed me to apply more wisdom and compassion to people's situations. Now only suburbia remained for us to experience as a family.

During these years, I continued my spiritual work with Master John. At the beginning it was very exciting. Other students also moved to the area from various places, and we were all glad to have the opportunity to learn from this teacher. Most of us were already deacons; some of us were not. Master John's style was different from Master Peter's because he was not the same person and had a different professional background, too. He was an engineer, and due to his scientific knowledge, he explained much of the cosmology in scientific terms. In essence the teachings were the same. They only differed in the style of presentation.

Over time, though, I got a sense that something was wrong. We had no new students coming to our center in Springfield, and very few new students were joining in the other centers, either. In 1989 Master Peter received inner Guidance that, as the order's director, he was to close the whole order down because it had become stagnant. He said it was meant to be a living organism, but instead it had become ingrown, and the ministers and priests were caught up in their own lives and personal concerns and were not drawing or serving anyone.

The news struck me like a bomb. What a blow! The other students and ministers expressed similar feelings. I had been totally convinced that I would be a part of this order for the rest of my life. Yes, I had noticed the lack of growth. I had also become aware of an apparent lack of harmony between the teachers. Though I registered these situations, I never imagined the order being gone. Even before the dissolution of the order, Master John increasingly decided to teach in a different way and with different lessons than those Master Peter was offering. He openly stated that he did not agree with how Master Peter was leading the order. I do not know what his specific complaints about the leadership were. I do know that once Master Peter dissolved the order, Master John declared complete autonomy. He told us the order was gone but that he would continue to teach us. We struggled to decipher what our new roles were. There seemed to be no form to contain us, but Master John continued teaching.

I was feeling very confused about my own spiritual development. I had thought that I was going there to be prepared for the priesthood, and yet I was not being prepared for it. Nor was I being offered ordination. Whenever I had a chance to talk with Master Peter, I asked him why this was the case. He said that he was not receiving inner guidance to ordain me. He was not sure why, but surely Jesus and Mary had a reason. Since no one offered me an explanation, I had plenty of time to come up with dozens of explanations by myself. I felt quite bad about myself, and was also confused by not having anyone tell me what I was doing wrong or inadequately. Initially, when we moved to Boston, I imagined that I would eventually begin a new midwifery practice there. Now, I thought I might be too attached to my midwifery and that was in the way of my becoming a priest. I did, indeed, love my work, but maybe I was too identified with it. So I decided that I must sacrifice it to make sure I loved God more. I did not practice midwifery for seven years after our move to New England.

I spent many hours and days trying to figure out what was wrong with me. How was I failing? I noticed that some other deacons who had not done nearly as much in terms of bringing in new students, teaching, baptizing, counseling, and Sunday services were becoming priests. If, as Jesus taught, it is by our fruits that we shall be known, why was I still being held back? Were my fruits not adequate evidence of my commitment, willingness, and ability to do this work? I wondered whether I wanted it too much. Or maybe I did not want it enough? Was I too proud or too ambitious? Was I too selfish or too pushy? Whenever I asked Master John, he had only vague answers for me. There was no vice I did not try myself for and no virtue I did not intensely seek to develop. Nothing seemed to make a difference. I drove to Springfield twice a week for years, and still I was a deacon who seemed to be stuck in neutral.

Master John's marriage was failing and it was taking a toll on him. We students did not realize what effect his state of mind and heart was having on us. We all seemed to be at a complete standstill in terms of growth, and most of us, according to him, were actually slipping backward. He told some students to stop attending some of the classes, and everyone, including myself, was feeling quite discouraged, even despondent. I don't know what was going on between Master John and the others, but his feedback to me became more and more negative. I sank into a deep depression. I had now been working with him for seven years, and I had never felt so badly about myself and so spiritually lost.

By 1993 my dreams were becoming increasingly ominous. Dream after dream portended doom. When I told Master John about the dreams, he agreed that the dreams were forecasting my death, but he provided no further indicator of what that meant. Were they predicting my spiritual death? This might prove beneficial if I needed to significantly change my life in order to move into the next stage. Or was it a spiritual death that indicated I was disconnecting from God? Was it physical death? Or the death of my walk upon this path? Master John only agreed with the seriousness of my situation without offering me any remedy.

The dreams finally deteriorated to the point that I felt as if a part of my soul was about to die. I was not only being drawn into Master John's deep depression, but he was projecting much of his anger and frustration at his wife onto me, and perhaps onto the other students as well. Though never prone to depression, I now felt near death. I started hearing statements like, "This has got to change! It must change!" coming up from my soul. I never lost contact with the God-Self in me, or I believe I might have just gone off the deep end. I got up all my courage and asked God within me the question I had been avoiding for quite some time, the previously unimaginable question: "Should I leave my teacher, Master John?"

It was the most frightening thing I had ever done. It was terrifying for several reasons: 1) I had built my life around these teachings and these people. 2) By now I knew that I had a vow on my soul to be a priest. I knew no other means by which I could become one, other than if Master John ordained me. Master Peter was not functioning outwardly as a teacher at the time, and I had no reason to believe he would do that again. 3) I knew that Master John would be angry with me for even asking the question. If I got the answer that I should leave him, he would not agree with that answer being right. He might, therefore, not allow me to be his student anymore. If I was wrong, I would have made an irreversible mistake that could cost me the chance to fulfill my life's purpose and my eternal vows.

The stakes were enormous. But I *had* to know God's will. If I asked guidance from God I knew I would have to be willing to follow what I was directed to do, no matter what that might be. Therefore, merely asking the question entailed taking the entire risk. I had to get the answer right. I went to my altar and prayed for a long while, asking Jesus and Mary to make me clear and strong so that I might hear the truth of God's will for me. Then I went into meditation. When I had gone deep inside and all was still, I asked, "Should I leave Master John and no longer be his student?"

I let myself stay in complete silence, as I awaited the answer. From within me I heard the Voice respond, "Yes, leave him." I did not know whether I was relieved that the torture of the past few years was about to end, or terrified of telling Master John and being on my own.

I called Master John that night and told him the guidance I had received. As I had anticipated, he told me I was wrong. I told him that I knew it was a possibility that I was wrong but I knew I had to follow my guidance, and I hoped God would have mercy on me for my obedience to it. He told me that he would not take me back as a student. I said that I was aware that I was taking that chance. When I got off the phone, my heart was pounding in my chest. I went to the chapel and fell on my knees in front of the altar.

"Did I do the right thing, oh God? Am I, in fact, in accord with your will in this matter?" Immediately I felt the heavens open up. I was flooded with light and angels came down and surrounded me and comforted me. My heart burst open with joy. "I was in accord! I was not wrong! Thank you God, thank you God!" This was Jesus' experience, too, when he went out to the desert to be tempted. When he resisted the last temptation, the angels came to him and ministered to him. I had resisted the biggest temptation I had ever faced. God knew nothing frightened me more than losing my chance at having a teacher, and never being

able to become the priest I had long ago vowed to be. This temptation was cus-
tom-made for me: I was put between the two things I valued most and was asked
to choose. Would I choose my teacher or would I choose the God-Self? If by following the God-Self I lost my teacher, would I still be obedient to the guidance?

The immense presence of light stayed with me for a few days. I had no idea
what would come next, but I knew I had been tested and I had chosen rightly. I
knew God was with me, and I needed only God. If I stayed close to the Self
within me, God would lead me to my next step. I gave praise and thanks daily,
hourly, while I simultaneously began to try to imagine where the path might take
me from there. A seven-year cycle was over. I had experienced highs, and I had
sunken lower than I had ever been before. I was now at a place of nothingness,
having nothing but God: no order, no teacher, no fellow ministers, and no students. I needed to regroup and find what I absolutely knew for myself, beyond
any shadow of a doubt.

God's Protection and Guidance Over the Students Who Trust

Many times people tell me that they would be too frightened to work with a
teacher because he or she might be a bad person or offer incorrect teachings.
What if they were obedient to someone who wasn't connected to God or had lost
connection with God? My teachers told me that if a teacher gets out of accord
with God and tells a student the wrong things to do, and the student does them,
then the student is blessed for his or her obedience to the teacher. The blame will
be on the teacher, not on the student. In my experience with Master John, I
gained firsthand knowledge of the truth of that teaching. Though I could not see
at the time why I had to go through all that pain and confusion, years later I came
to see that it was exactly the training I needed for my future position as a spiritual
leader and teacher. I needed to go through all those years of trying to figure out
why I was not being moved on into the priesthood. I needed to go through the
immense pain of not understanding and of no one else having the answers, either.
I needed to go through the abyss of working with a teacher who was depressed so
that I could experience what happens when teachers let their personal pain infil-
trate their teaching and their relationships with students. I needed to be tested in
the most trying way to see whether I would be obedient to God, even if it cost me
what I held most dear. Finally, I needed to be spiritually entirely alone, without
an order, to evaluate what I knew, *for an absolute fact*, within my own being.

Many a time, I have been able to tell this story to students to comfort them when they have been afraid of such a situation. I have told them that they can rest assured that if I am wrong in what I direct them to do, and they follow my instruction, than nothing but grace will fall upon them, and I will be the one who has to face the consequences. I am so glad to know this because it also comforts me in that I know my students are protected from any errors I might make. I will gladly answer for them rather than cause one of them any harm. God's loving kindness established such a wise system to guide us and care for us along the way. The innocent are blessed. Those who have the greater knowing are held responsible for more. I always pray to God that He/She may guide me in all that I do so I may lead the students that God gives me with wisdom and in accord with God's will for them. I am happy to know that God will straighten me out swiftly and clearly if I begin to slide, for this is my prayer, and God always answers our prayers.

The Husband's Heart Attack

In 1991 I began a new midwifery practice after a seven-year break. I felt good working with women again in this blessed way. Massachusetts turned out to be a positive place for direct entry midwifery, which is the practice of midwifery by those who are not nurses. I submitted my home-birth midwife credentials to the Massachusetts Midwifery Association, along with a full packet of data on births attended, complications I had managed, documented outcomes, and recommendation letters from doctors and midwives who knew my work. In return, this professional organization certified me as a midwife, as did a national organization a few years later. I became a Certified Professional Midwife in this state where it was legal to practice. I teamed up with another midwife named Heather, and since she had a busy practice, I was quickly back in the habit of attending a full schedule of births.

One night during a major snowstorm, Heather phoned to say that we had been called to a birth that was an hour south of my house. She said it might take her a while to get to me due to the snowstorm, but she would be there to pick me up as soon as she could. She did take about 45 minutes instead of the usual 25. When I started to climb into her van, we realized that neither of us had directions to the woman's house, which was highly unusual for both of us. We went back into the house to call the family, and to our amazement, they informed us that the baby had just been born and that they were all doing fine. They had a nurse there with them, and told us not to hurry because the roads were so treacherous.

While we were getting this surprising information, Sal came halfway down the steps, then sat on a step. He looked strange. I turned to him and said, "What?" I thought he was going to complain about the noise we were making. Instead he told me that he was having trouble breathing and he felt a lot of pressure on his chest. Heather and I both knew those were signs of a possible heart attack. Though we both thought it was unlikely that he was having one, Heather told me to stay with Sal and care for him, since the baby was already born. I was hesitant to let her drive alone in the storm, but she assured me that she would be careful. As she walked out she hollered, "Have him chew on an aspirin, just in case."

I knew the protocol for such symptoms was to call an ambulance. Sal reluctantly agreed. Firefighters arrived first; they traipsed in wearing all their noisy fire suits. They took Sal out on a stretcher. I followed the ambulance to the hospital. Ten minutes after we arrived at the hospital, Sal went into a full cardiac arrest while I stood by his side, watching in horror. He was without a pulse for three minutes, was revived by CPR, cussed, and went out again for two more minutes. They had to apply the paddles three times, and they pounded his chest more than once. At that time I was still working with Master John, so I ran out and called him immediately, even while they were still reviving Sal. Master John told me later that he went straight to his chapel and prayed for Sal. He saw Sal pass over to the other side, where his father met him and told him that he needed to return to take care of his children. When Sal came to, he had no memory of the time he was unconscious. Only the paddle burns and fist-bruises on his chest made him believe that his heart had actually stopped. However, he was very teary that day and told me that he was thinking a lot about his father and our kids.

Sal recovered amidst the kids and I feeling very grateful for how well we had been taken care of. If there had not been a snowstorm, Heather would have come sooner. We would have been gone when Sal started having symptoms. If we had had directions in the car, we would also have been gone. If we had not made noise that woke Sal up, he might have died in his sleep. If the baby had not already been born, I might have been tempted to go with Heather rather than stay with Sal, since it seemed so unlikely that he, at age 45, would be having a heart attack. Sal himself said that he would most likely not have called an ambulance, and I therefore would have found him dead upon my return from the birth. I was meant to be there with him, and God brought about a whole series of events that led to saving Sal's life.

Sal's heart attack introduced an entirely new element into our family life. The doctors told him that if he did not stop smoking and watch his diet and lifestyle, he could expect another heart attack within five years. Next time, he would not be likely to walk away from it. Sal tried to stop smoking on his own but would not humble himself to go to a group or get more help. He continued to smoke, and he ate whatever he wanted. The kids and I tried every possible way to get him to stop smoking and to eat right. We begged and pleaded, we yelled and threatened, we cried and grieved. Finally, I realized that it was not my job to heal him. That was *his* job. It was my job to love him, and he would make his own choices about his life. Once I caught on to this, the children followed suit. From that time on, we knew his days were numbered. It was a sad fact that we had to learn to live with, and in many ways we began grieving his virtually certain death.

Sal became seriously ill numerous times over the following years. Sometimes the trouble was in his lungs, sometimes his heart, and sometimes his digestive system. He was immensely afraid of doctors and hospitals due to bad experiences he had had as a child. As many men do, he expressed that fear in a way that looked much more like anger and disdain than fear. The first few times he got very ill after the heart attack, I felt like I had to take him to the hospital even if I had to talk him into it. His response to my doing so was to blame me for his having to endure whatever they did to him there. Each time my diagnosis of what was going on with him was correct, and each time I urged him to go to the hospital, he was, in fact, experiencing a life-threatening health problem. He gave me such a hard time for taking him in that I felt at a loss about what to do with him.

On the night of my fortieth birthday, Sal was having increasing trouble breathing. His complexion turned a yellowish green, and each breath sounded worse than the one before. I dreaded another scene. As I was about to go to bed, I prayed that God intervene and that I be shown a way to stop the cycle. I heard from within me: "He will not die tonight." This answer I heard was so clear that I had no doubt of its truth. I thought, "Well, if he is not going to die tonight, I can let him do whatever he wants." A great part of my fear the previous times had been that if I did not insist on getting emergency care when he needed it, and he then died, the kids would feel angry at me. This event, however, was different, because I knew for sure that this was not his night to die. Having that knowledge allowed me to maintain equanimity, which I certainly could not have done otherwise. I felt that God was answering my prayer for help to somehow change this emotional jam I kept finding myself in when Sal became seriously ill. With that feeling of equanimity, I could even chuckle a bit to myself as I watched Sal's surprise at the absence of my usual responses to his illnesses.

Sal, on the other hand, felt for the first time that he was, in fact, going to die. He could not believe that I was going to go to sleep when he was doing so poorly. He kept waiting until I was almost asleep to say something or ask me for something. Once he said, "It would not be very nice of me to die on your birthday, would it?" I agreed that it would not. When he woke me, I asked whether he needed something. He said no, and I dozed off again. Once he asked, "Do you think oxygen might help?" I told him I thought it would help some. He asked, "Would you be willing to get the oxygen tank you have for births and let me use it?" I got it, put the mask on him, and went back to bed. A while later he asked, "Do you think I need to go to the hospital?"

I said, somewhat tongue-in-cheek, "A general rule of thumb might be that when one is having trouble breathing, a hospital would be the location of choice." He laughed, responding to my humor, though his fear was becoming more evident. He got out his checkbooks and wrote blank checks for me to use when he died. He wrote down the whereabouts of all his assets and put some other papers in order. He asked me how I would manage the mortgage payments if he died.

"This is one fine time to think of that, Sal!"

He strained to laugh again.

After he stopped trying to get me to say he should go to the hospital, I finally told him that if he wanted me to do anything, such as call the doctor or take him to the hospital, he would have to ask me *really* nicely. Once I took him, he would have to express how grateful he was that I had taken him in and was now staying there with him. Soon after, he did ask me very nicely to please call the doctor and tell him that he was going to the hospital. He was grateful for my help and expressive of that gratitude.

From that night on, the tables were turned in terms of how we related regarding his health issues. He became gracious and kind, and we worked well together whenever we needed to. All of this would not have been possible if God had not given me the absolute certainty that Sal was not going to die that night while simultaneously giving Sal the fear that he would. I was amazed at God's creativity in answering my plea for help, and at God's humor in addressing the situation.

11

THE PRIESTHOOD: ORDINATION, SERVICE, AND FORMING AN ORDER

If you bring forth what is within you,
What is within you will save you.
If you do not bring forth what is within you,
What is within you will destroy you.

—Rabbi Nochman,
from Martin Buber's *The Tales of the Hasidism,* 1948

Sojourn Into Catholicism and Beginning Jungian Psychology Training

I had been working with teachers for so long that I hardly knew what to do with myself when I did not have one. As I found myself in this new void where there was just God and me, I wondered what to do next. One of my teachers had told me about a military strategy that applied to being on the spiritual path. He said that when a group of soldiers finds themselves in a situation where they have more ground than they can defend, they often pull back to a smaller territory, one that they *know* they can defend. I felt like I was now in such a situation. What did I actually know, beyond a shadow of a doubt? What could I defend to the death? There was no order anymore. I had no teacher. Without any such structure, teachings, or practices to contain me, what was entirely mine? What had become a part of me, no matter what teachings were or were not available to structure it all?

I decided to go back to the most basic of all things: Did I *really* know for a fact that God exists? At first it was frightening to even allow myself to question this, the most fundamental notion. I had to consider what I would do if I found out the answers to such questions were "no," and decided that I did want to know, even if the answers were that utterly disturbing. So I went into meditation and asked myself the question: Do I know beyond a shadow of a doubt that God is? The answer came welling up inside me with such power and joy: "Yes! Yes! And forever yes!" The presence of God within me filled me to such an extent that I broke into laughter at the silliness of even asking such a question. It was more absurd than asking whether I was sure I was in a physical body.

Having settled that question, I asked, "Do I know that I see God within me and that I hear God speaking to me?" I thought back over the many times I had received inner guidance, followed it, and had wondrous things happen that I could have never planned or even known about. The evidence was overwhelming that the voice inside me had never been wrong. Did I know that I had direct contact inside me? I recalled my first face-to-face meeting with God when I was brought into Self-realization, followed by many, many encounters since, and I knew without a doubt that I did have a direct visual, auditory, thinking, and feeling relationship with that Oneness.

So I knew my initiations were real and I knew that God was real. What did I know for sure about Jesus and Mary? I knew they were real beings, and I knew they loved me, guided me, and spoke to me. I had experienced their healing power in myself and in others. I also knew that it was due to Their working in and through the orders I had been exposed to that the people in those orders carried such light in their beings. All the other teachings about Mary and Jesus were not firsthand knowledge, so I did not include them in what I knew for certain.

What did I know about real teachers? I knew that they could, in fact, initiate a person into realities he or she would otherwise have no access to. I knew they had experienced those realities personally and could therefore help a student move toward them swiftly. I also knew that teachers could get lost, just like anyone else could, and that when teachers got lost, their students could suffer. But with that knowing came the knowledge that I had been protected and guided even during that period in which Master John was not functioning well due to his depression. I still had a sense that it had all been purposeful. Someday I would know why I had to have that experience and what I was to learn from it.

One other thing I felt I knew for sure was that it is wonderful to be a part of a true spiritual order. Having had a spiritual training school and the opportunity to grow alongside other students who made similar commitments had been such a joy and a great help on my path. I learned from other people's mistakes, and I learned from their achievements and successes. I saw how God could work through such orders to teach many people at once from one situation, yet all could experience the lesson as tailor-made for them alone. I was still sad that Master Peter had disbanded the order and hoped and prayed that some day I would find and be able to join another order.

All in all, I knew that I had a real relationship with God, whom I could see and hear, and whom I trusted implicitly. I knew my initiations were real, my teachers had been real, and that a holy order provides wonderful opportunities to those who join it that would otherwise not be available. Having tallied up those factors, I asked myself what I should do now. I missed having communion and sharing in Sunday services, so I went to try to find a church to join. I asked to speak to the priest at a Catholic parish that was recommended to me. I met with a Father Michael and told him my spiritual life story. When I finished he said, "It sounds like you have the contents, and all you need is the form." I felt this priest had really understood and respected what I had told him. I asked whether I could join the church, but he said he did not think I would like it and suggested I attend a service there and then meet with him again.

I attended mass the next day. It was a lively congregation that sang heartily and well. But there were indeed things that appalled me. They allowed the children to run around the altar, and even jump up on it after the service. I held altars in high respect, and my children would never approach one without behaving respectfully. The congregation also used the point in the mass that is called the peace blessing—where one shakes the hands of the people all around one's own seat and says "peace be with you"—as a time to exchange recipes and make golf dates. And when I saw the priest lift up the chalice and paten for the transmutation into Jesus' body and blood, he seemed to be unconvinced of the power of that moment.

After the mass I met with Father Michael. He wanted to know what bothered me. I told him about the altar and the peace blessing. He smiled and said, "I thought you might not like it very much."

Then I asked him, "Father, do you know, for a fact, that the transmutation occurs?"

He became quiet. "Do you?" he asked.

"Yes, Father, I see it happen."

"Did it happen this morning?"

"Yes, I saw the blessing descend on it." The way Father Michael looked at me told me that he believed that I saw it.

"Would you let me know when you see it happen?" he asked. I agreed, and from then on when he held up the chalice during a mass, he looked at me, and when I saw it transmute, I nodded. He also came and sought me out during the peace blessing, and we gave each other a solemn blessing with our handshake. Based on his recommendation, I did not join the Roman Church. He told me that if my conscience allowed me to receive communion, he saw it as his duty to serve me. I told him my conscience absolutely approved of my receiving communion. We agreed that I would not tell people in the congregation that I was not Catholic because some might have a problem with my taking communion. I attended this church for more than a year.

A few months after ending my relationship with Master John, I searched for things to read that might help me understand what had happened to me while I was with him. I read some women's psychology books and wondered about women's spiritual development. My question was whether spiritual development is inherently different for women than it is for men. I came across the writings of a Jungian analyst named Marion Woodman. Many things that she said gave me much insight into my struggles with Master John. My readings also made me wonder whether there existed a psychological language and theory that encompassed the mystical. As I read more Jungian writings, I became increasingly intrigued with the prospect that this discipline might be inclusive to both psychology and mysticism. I discovered that there was a Jungian Training Institute in Boston. Upon inquiring, they told me that I needed to have a masters degree, preferably in psychology, to even apply. Only a few students were accepted into training each year.

I was on fire with enthusiasm to learn more. I felt Master John might have been a better teacher if he had studied more psychology. He might also have recognized his own depression sooner and understood the phenomena of projection and counter-transference. In projection, one projects one's issues onto another person. In counter-transference, a minister or counselor type succumbs to the student or client's projection (usually of a parental figure) onto the teacher/counselor. The teacher/counselor then also begins to lose ground in helping the student/client. Without knowledge of this phenomenon that both Jung and Freud studied and described, things can get very confused. Master Peter was a psychologist, and I felt that helped him in many ways as a teacher, hence all my interest in learning Jungian psychology.

At the time I had not finished my bachelor's degree. I inquired and found that Cambridge College offered a program for adults like me who needed to finish their undergraduate work. I began my studies there in 1993 and received a Masters in Counseling Psychology with a specialty in Marriage and Family Therapy in 1996. The Jungian Institute wanted their applicants to have received at least

100 hours of analysis with a Jungian analyst before they applied for training. In the spring of 1996, I began weekly sessions with a woman analyst who lived nearby. I was mostly interested in learning about dream interpretation and psychological complexes. I was not there to get to know myself better, as I felt I had been intensively doing that kind of introspective work for many years. I did, however, want to get to know the language of Jungian psychology and how it applied to my inner experiences. I longed to understand dream symbolism. I also wanted to know whether Carl Jung's definitions of Self and Soul were the same as the mystical definitions I was familiar with.

In 1997, I was admitted to the analyst-training program at the Boston Jung Institute and embarked on my studies that fall. I also began a small private psychotherapy practice alongside my midwifery practice. I counseled individuals and couples, both short-term and long-term. I generally found myself enjoying counseling work but felt it was greatly lacking without the spiritual element that I knew to be essential to human health and happiness. Most of my clients were not interested in the spiritual, so I offered them what counseling psychology has to offer.

Master Peter Re-Enters My Life and Gives Ordination into the Priesthood

I had been talking with Master Peter on the phone once every few months or so, beginning several months after I stopped working with Master John. I was still burnt out from my years with Master John, and it took Master Peter and I many conversations over a number of months to establish a means of relating that worked for us. He came to the east coast for a vacation in 1995 and stayed with Sal and me for three days. We had conversations about what had and had not worked in the Brotherhood of Christ. He was speaking from the teacher and director perspective, and I was talking from the student and deacon perspective. We had some heated discussions in which we tried to re-establish a relationship that was outside the boundaries of an order and therefore also outside the confines of a teacher/student relationship. He was sympathetic to the pain I had experienced and sorry it had happened that way. He was also open to hearing my perspective on what could have been done differently.

In early October 1996, I had lost Master Peter's e-mail address and therefore needed to send him a "snail-mail" letter to request it. In that letter I told him a dream I had had of him the previous night. Master Peter called me the day after he received the letter and asked me what I thought the dream meant. He had also studied Jungian dream interpretation for a number of years and worked with dreams daily in his thriving psychotherapy practice. I had already discussed the dream with my analyst and had received a good Jungian interpretation, which I shared with Master Peter. After giving him my insights, I asked what he thought it meant.

He said, "I see it telling me that I should offer you ordination as a priest."

I was stunned beyond words. When I recovered my ability to speak, I asked, "Have you forgotten there is no order to ordain me into?"

He said, "I know. You would be on your own, without an order."

"Is that ever done?" I asked.

"Not usually. But this is the inner guidance I am getting. God must have something in mind for you. Of course, it is only an offer. You do not need to accept it."

Master Peter and I agreed that I would take three days to meditate and con-template what I wanted, and to seek inner guidance regarding his offer. After the three days were up, I called him and told him I accepted. Master Peter asked guidance for the date of the ordination, and he began giving me instructions regarding preparations. He also sent me several books I was to read and suggested meditations and prayers that would help prepare me. I was to be secluded and fasting for the three days immediately prior to my ordination. I needed a priest's chasuble, which is a kind of a cloak, to wear over my simple white deacon's alb. I needed a decorative white rope called a cincture to tie at my waist. Master Peter sent me molds to have a priest's ring and a cross made. I set up a chapel room in my home. I invited friends and some family to join me for my ordination and the feast that was to follow. Sal agreed to cook for everyone. Twenty-five people accepted the invitation, which was the limit of what my chapel could hold. Almost all of these people had no idea what this was about, but they came because they were either curious or cared about me. The three days before a priest is ordained in this tradition are to be spent in seclusion and fasting. I found a Jesuit monastery nearby that agreed to rent me a quiet room for my three days of seclusion. Master Peter told me before I went into the seclusion that my assign-ment was to "die unto myself." This was to be the time of my crucifixion into God. I was to give over my entire mind, heart, body, and soul to God. This is the "Crucifixion of the Lamb" that the New Testament refers to, in which one lays one's heart and mind on the altar and sacrifices them to God.

My three days in seclusion were not at all as I expected. I alternated between sleeping and waking for periods of a few hours. Much of my time was put into prayer and meditation. I had only the Bible and the text of the ordination sacrament to read. My deacon ordination had been 12 years ago. All the difficult feelings of those years—the hurt, the anger, and the confusion—came up and would not go away. I struggled to get to the bottom of it all but the negative feelings grew. On the last night, Master Peter arrived in Boston and came to see me at the monastery. He found me in an intense state of hurt and anger. He asked me whether I thought I was going to find resolution by morning, and I told him I hoped so. He suggested that at some time I might also want to ask guidance regarding what I was to do with this priesthood—how I was to serve.

The night felt like the greatest battle of my life. I prayed and struggled to understand why I could not clear all these intense negative feelings. I wanted to know what was I to do to give over my life to God. Around three a.m., during my sleep, I was told to get up and read the vows I was going to take the next day. I knew this directive came from the God-Self. I got up and reread the vows. They were to be vows of poverty, humility, obedience, service, and chastity. I felt the movement of the Spirit heightening my awareness to a crystal-clear state. All the noise in me stopped. Then, before my eyes unfolded the meaning of the vows and what I was to give over:

- Poverty: I was to have no Gods before the one God, the Self within me. That was to be my only treasure and was to matter to me above all else.

- Humility: I was to have the humility to bow to God alone and to accept God's directives as true and good without caring about my own opinions on the matter.

- Obedience: I was to be totally obedient to God-within.

- Service: I was to serve only God and the people God gave me to serve.

- Chastity: I was to be chaste, i.e. pure in my complete giving over to God, as pure as Mother Mary, who gave Herself over to carry the Christ within her being.

A beautiful, still peace came over me, the stillness after the storm. Was I willing to take these five vows and give myself over to God with my entire being? Yes, I was. In this altered state of pure clarity, as I accepted the vows God was offering me, I saw unveiled before me the entire path I had trod to arrive at this place. I saw how every piece fit in place to bring me to the dawn of this, my ordination day. God had been guiding and teaching me through all the joys and all the sorrows. God would surely lead me on from here.

Still in this state of peace, I asked Self the question Master Peter had suggested I ask, "How does God want me to serve Him/Her as a priest?"

The answer came swiftly and clearly, "Start a women's order."

I was absolutely stunned. "Was that even possible?" I asked myself. "Don't you need to be a master teacher to start an order?" In all the years in which I had longed to be a part of another order, I had never thought that I would be the person to start one. I assumed it would have to be one of the teachers from the Brotherhood of Christ. As I pondered this, I was hit with the next thought, "What will Master Peter think when I tell him about this guidance? Won't he think that I am arrogant to believe that I can be ordained a priest and right away start an order?" I decided to put that guidance on the back burner and revisit it later. I had been taught to check my guidance carefully several times over, especially when the questions are major ones. There was no question about whether I would obey the guidance, only a question of whether I was sure that this was, indeed, God's will for me.

Morning arrived. I packed up my things and drove back to my house. I was to maintain silence except for talking with the teachers. Master Peter was very glad to see and hear that I had come through my valley of darkness and death and was clearly peaceful and prepared for ordination. I felt amazement at the process I had been taken through. I had sweated, wept, cried out, and fumed with anger for much of the three days of my seclusion. I had been struggling with my own resistance to dying completely to all I had held of value and to everything that I had perceived myself to be until this point in my life. My new life was to be contained in those five vows, and in them alone was I to find peace. I felt radiant and blessed with inner stillness and awe at God's amazing love, which had guided me through my death into new life. This felt like it completed the death that had begun with my choosing to be obedient to my inner guidance even when it cost me my teacher. Now I had given over all to the God-Self within. I had no idea what my life would become, but I was filled with peace and the knowing that God was guiding me.

A three-hour silent meditation took place before the ordination. Once the ordination began, Master Peter and I were clearly in an entirely different realm from all the people who had come to witness this sacrament. Master Peter confirmed this later when I told him of that feeling. He said this sacrament takes place on the other side of the veil, in the heaven world. Time feels different there, the meaning and sound of words is different, and I could feel the presence of some of the great ones there with us. The ordination went very smoothly. As I took my vows joy filled me. Master Peter placed the priest's ring on my finger, marrying me for all eternity to God. This is the great marriage through the eternal vows of the priesthood. He hung a silver and gold priest's cross around my neck on a blue ribbon, symbolizing the path I represent, under Whom I work, and as a reminder of the great gift Jesus gave us through His death. Master Peter put the priest's chasuble on me, symbolizing the yoke of light under the high priests of our order, Jesus and Mary. He knotted a white cincture around my waist, symbolizing that I was now tied to this ministry. I was to live it in purity, and I was given the authority of the priesthood. As holy, sacred words were spoken with each action of the ordination, I felt lifted up into the hosts above and welcomed into the great conclave of the servants of the most high, under Jesus Christ and Mother Mary. Master Peter called down a blessing of protection and supply for all my needs, and proclaimed that what I would give would be returned to me one hundred-fold.

Sometimes new names are given at baptism, sometimes they're given when one is ordained as a deacon, and sometimes they're not given at all. My name had not been changed on these prior occasions, and I had no particular feelings about it potentially being changed now. Toward the end of the ordination rite, Master Peter told me that my new name was to be Reverend Clare. I was amazed because I had not given much more thought to the guidance I had gotten regarding starting a women's order. I had not told Master Peter, and I planned to meditate more on it to make sure it was truly guided. When I heard my new name, Clare, the first thought that came to my mind was that Saint Clare of Assisi formed one of the first and longest-lasting women's orders in history. Did this mean that I had heard correctly, and was actually to go ahead with forming a women's order? It was such an amazing thought that I had to set it aside while I continued with the rest of the ordination.

The rite ended with Master Peter giving me the bishop's kiss on the top of my head as I knelt. I had not noticed how out of this world I had been until I turned and saw all the faces of people eager to hug and congratulate me. They looked as though they had felt something important was going on but could not make heads or tails of most of it. I was not sure how I was going to talk with anyone. I accepted their hugs and good wishes and went downstairs with them to partake of the feast that Sal had cooked for us. As I stood talking with everyone, I felt the conversations were surrealistic. When I met Master Peter's eyes, I knew he recognized the world I was still in, and that he was there, too. It seemed strange that everyone else was in a fairly regular earthly realm and not aware of the heavenly realm that was still upon us.

Forming New Orders for Women and for Men

The next morning, I continued to feel so off the Earth that I searched for some way to bring myself down so I could function in normal life. I shared breakfast with Master Peter, and was looking for all the foods that might ground me in my physical body. I said, "By the way, I did ask that guidance question about how I was to serve in this priesthood."

"What answer did you get?" he asked.

I gathered up all my courage and said, "I got the guidance that I was to start a women's order."

I expected him to say something about what a fat head I had, for I was ordained less than a day yet I wanted to start an order. Instead, to my great surprise, he said, "I am not surprised. Well, when you get your order started, if you want me to, I will be glad to come teach some classes." We hugged goodbye and he was gone. I stood there with my mouth hanging open, not quite comprehending what had just happened. Did he just express agreement and support that I was to start a women's order?

I went home and pondered how I might begin. I meditated, prayed, got guidance to consult with Beatrice and Nancy W., two women whom I had trained as midwives and who had been at my ordination. They might be interested or know someone else who would. I invited both of them to come to my house, but I did not tell them what I wished to talk about. When they arrived, I expressed my astonishment that they had come without asking what this meeting was for. They said that in their minds I had earned the right to ask such a thing of them. They trusted and respected me so much. I was moved by their sentiment and emboldened to lay my story and my question out to them.

I told them about the other two orders, and what I had experienced—the great blessings as well as the problems. I also told them that I was told to start a women's order. I asked whether they would be interested in being a part of such a spiritual training school and sisterhood. Both women were deeply moved. One wept as she said, "All my life I have waited for such a thing. Yes, with all my heart, yes!" We discussed inviting other women, making a mission statement, the format of classes, and holding Sunday services. We were lifted into such a high and inspired state when we spoke that three hours had passed by the time we checked our watches (we all guessed it had only been one).

That coming Sunday was the first day of Advent, the season most associated with Mother Mary. What more appropriate day could there be to inaugurate a new women's order and spiritual school? I asked God what I was to name this order and was told to call it The Holy Order of Sophia. The word "Sophia" is the Greek word for wisdom and is often used to refer to a feminine face or aspect of God. I was delighted that it was to be the name of the order, though I felt a bit daunted by the "Holy" part of the name. But I rechecked the guidance and was told from within that that was, in fact, to be the name. Only the three of us were there that first Sunday morning. I gave my first sermon as a priest and served priest communion for the first time. Beatrice and Nancy said they felt good about it all, though this form of a service was quite unfamiliar to both of them.

I started teaching classes once each week, too. I had written my master's thesis on mysticism and women just a few months before, so I had virtually every book ever authored that related to women's spirituality right there on my bookshelf. I went back to a number of them to help me decide how I was going to teach these women and how I was going to help them develop spiritually. Each class became somewhat experimental, as I tried out many different exercises and meditations from various books. Over the next few months, other women joined our group and enjoyed the eclectic mixture of paths and teachings that I was presenting. I talked with Master Peter once a month and told him what we were doing. He offered any assistance I might want, since he had led an order before, but was very respectful of my doing it my own way. A couple of times, he asked whether I had considered using the lessons and exercises from the Brotherhood of Christ. I told him that I thought there was better and more interesting material to work with that was more suited to women. He mentioned that I might want to try the former order material again and see how it worked.

I continued with the eclectic mixture of teachings for over a year. I had a group of half a dozen women who came regularly. In spite of all our efforts, and many classes that were inspiring and interesting, it was painfully obvious to me that my students were not carrying any more light in their beings, and they were not being transformed the way I had seen it happen in the Brotherhood. When I voiced my puzzlement over this to Master Peter, he suggested that maybe I should reconsider my avoidance of the order writings and exercises. I told him that they were outdated, the language was terrible, and they used male pronouns for God. How could I use such material? Master Peter said, "I could rewrite them and update them. Would that help?"

I answered, "It would certainly help, and if you rewrite them I will try using them. But I am not convinced that will make a difference."

Within the next few weeks, Master Peter rewrote the book the Brotherhood called "The Tree of Life" and I began using it as a teaching book. I also invited him to come and teach a workshop there in Boston. He came for the first workshop weekend in June 1997. About a dozen people sat in my living room and listened to him talk about discipleship. That was to be the first in a tradition of monthly workshops that we offered in Boston and which, from then on, Master Peter and I co-taught. He had, in that same month, started teaching weekly classes once again in Milwaukee. In November of that year, he invited me to join him in teaching a workshop to his students in Milwaukee. While there, I learned that his students really had no idea of the power of a master teacher since he had not said anything about it. I informed them that he was a master teacher—one who had not only come through the three great initiations of baptism, illumination, and Self-realization himself, but had also been trained and empowered to bring other people into those initiations. When master teachers hold the rights of ordination, they can also ordain priests into the true priesthood that is overseen by Jesus and Mary. There are not very many master teachers at any given time on the earth, and a person who has the opportunity to learn from one would do well to make good use of that opportunity.

Master Peter and I spent long hours discussing how we might work together. We cleared up many concerns I had about how we could prevent the problems that had occurred in the other orders from recurring here. We spoke of feminist psychology and values, and of how any of that might have a place in our work as priests. We spoke at length about teacher/student relationships, about integrity, and about our goals for our students. Since I was now using the lessons and spiritual exercises from the prior orders, I was, to my own surprise, seeing obvious and impressive growth in my students. I could not deny that there was, in fact, something amazing in this method that I had not been able to bring about for my students using any other materials. It was purported that these teachings were written alchemically, meaning they had been assembled in such a way that they would have a very specific effect on the students, bringing them into a state of preparedness for illumination. I had never given too much credence to these claims before. Now I saw evidence that spoke for itself.

Clearly, having Master Peter co-teach the workshops each month was making a big difference. Before long, some students were ready for illumination. Master Peter taught me how to bring them into this state of being filled with light. I was amazed to be learning this and to be given the great gift of being able to bring it to others. I was now truly learning to work on the other side of the veil, where this work is done in the spiritual world and in the spiritual body. My students were thrilled and could not get enough of the new and wonderful grace that came through these teachings.

Marcella was my third student and had been faithfully coming since the second month of my teaching classes. Now her husband, Tim, wanted to come, too. He did not mind being the only man. Suddenly, we were no longer women only. The other women had nothing against him being there, since he did not have the option to receive these teachings in another setting. How could it be right to exclude him based on gender?

I began co-teaching workshops with Master Peter in Milwaukee as he also did with me in Boston. Our working relationship became quite smooth and enjoyable. We laughed a lot and worked as partners in getting these teachings out to the people. Many of his students in Milwaukee were women, so they enjoyed seeing an example of a woman taking on spiritual authority.

In April 1999, Master Peter and I formed and incorporated an order for men and women and called it The Order of Christ/Sophia. We were co-directors of this order and received guidance to continue with both orders for the time being. My first student, Beatrice, was ordained a deacon, and in June 1999, we ordained four more deacons at our first annual summer retreat: Marcella from Boston and three women from Milwaukee. At that same summer retreat, Master Peter laid his hands on my head after one morning communion and blessed me into beginning my training toward becoming a master teacher. I was now no longer just a priest, but what was called a sister teacher. The blessing was powerful, and I knew another stage of my spiritual life and service had begun.

12

LIFE IN GOD: CELIBACY, LOVE, AND BECOMING A MASTER TEACHER

Only when we renounce the world completely can we go behind the veil to be surrounded in royal purple. Only when we have cut our ties with earth can we travel from infinity to infinity. Only when we release the dross of material consciousness will we take our place above the angels, the rightful place of the priest. All this and more is given to the one who will love the Creator above all things. If we hold anything before our Creator…it will turn to ashes. This is because when you have become a priest you are functioning on a higher level of realization now, and the only support of your power and authority is God. Your mind and intention has to be pure, including all of the subtleties of mind, feeling, and emotion. This means that you will place God first over all you desire, all that you like and want to do, and all that you don't want to do.

—Father Paul Blighton, *Manual of Sacramental Initiation,* 1968

End of Married Life and Death of Husband

Beginning in the summer of 1998, Sal and I had serious and intense conversations about what we each saw ourselves doing for the rest of our lives, now that our youngest child, Sofia, was about to graduate from high school. Sal said he felt sure that he needed to live in Italy. He had bought a 10-acre olive grove on a mountain in Southern Italy the year before. He felt remorse that he had run away from his family when he moved to the USA at 24. His siblings had trouble getting along with each other, and Sal now wanted to try to bring peace into their relationships. He said he did not know how much longer he had on Earth, and he felt living in Italy was essential for him.

I, on the other hand, knew for a fact that I did not need to live on a remote mountain in Italy. At age 46, I knew I needed to get ever more deeply involved in my ministry. I needed to be in cities where there were people to teach and serve. Sal and I both felt stunned by the scenario that was unfolding before us. We were having deep and caring conversations about our feelings, needs, and desires. In fact, we were communicating better than we ever had before. Sal knew from the beginning of these talks that it was highly unlikely that I would want to go with him. He opened the talks knowing that he would need to do this by himself. Yet he felt his journey was so imperative that if it meant leaving the marriage, he would have to do so.

In March 1999, I asked for inner guidance about whether we were to end our marriage and go our separate ways. The answer was a resounding "yes." I was still seeing my Jungian analyst once a week, as was required for me to be a student at the Jung Institute. She was deeply disturbed at the prospect of breaking up a marriage of 28 years that was actually functioning well, and was concerned that we were making a big mistake. I had not had any dreams that shed light on the matter, so I told her that I would ask for one.

Sal was to leave for Italy in early April. The last night we were together, I had a dream in which I was outdoors. Sal was just a few yards away. He called me with an urgent sound in his voice to come look at something. I went to him and looked up toward where he was pointing. In the sky just above us was a large, beautiful angel who was singing, "Glory to God in the highest!" The sky then filled with angels, all singing along with the first one. The cause for their rejoicing was clearly our upcoming divorce. That was the end of my dream. I asked my analyst, "Is that good enough, or do you need God to speak?" She laughed and said that she was more than satisfied that the dream was indicative of our decision being a good one.

Sal left as scheduled in early April, and during his return visit in June, we finalized the divorce. It was simple and straightforward, for we agreed on all the issues. In an atmosphere of respect and fairness, we even left financial assets to each other that we could have rightfully laid claim to. It was clean and amicable, though there was an element of sadness and astonishment at how this had all come about. I wondered whether Sal was going home to die. Several people echoed that thought to me. That did, in fact, turn out to be the case. Only 16 months after moving to Italy, Sal died suddenly of a massive heart attack while in his little house in the olive grove. He had had enough time to try to settle his family disputes and to discover that such resolution was not possible. He had reconnected with the Italian soil and culture, settled his affairs with everyone, and left his physical body in September 2000. He is buried in Italy in the same cemetery as his parents. It felt very clear that Sal and I were to raise four kids, and then we were done. It did not feel wrong, but rather supremely ordered and right.

Another Priest, Founding of a Novice Program, and Celibacy Vows

In the fall of 1999, Master Peter ordained Beatrice, my first student, into the priesthood. Only master teachers who have been given ordination rights can ordain someone into the priesthood. Ordination into priesthood is a very serious matter, and it is the responsibility of the ordaining master to make sure that the ordination of this person is God's will and that he or she is adequately prepared. After the ordination, the new priest continues to be trained and supported throughout his or her priesthood. The students and deacons in Milwaukee and also in Boston were excited to have the first priest ordained into the new order. The deacons from Milwaukee drove to Boston and joined in the solemnities and the celebration of this joyful event.

Beatrice moved in with me after Sal left for Italy that previous spring. My home now turned into an order house, with most of the comings and goings centered around our ministry. I still had my midwifery and psychotherapy offices on the lower floor, and the rooms doubled as classrooms for the spirituality classes. In August we got inner guidance to start a live-in novice program for women. Three single women in their twenties who had become serious students over the past months or year jumped at the opportunity to be the first novices in training. One of them was my daughter Pascale. I rearranged some of the rooms in the house, and the three young women moved in mid-September. The purpose of the women's novice program was to give women a chance to live intensively in spiritual community, learning to become strong as people, strong in their relational skills to others, and strong in their closeness to God. They had the advantages of having daily communion and evening prayers right there in the house. They also had access to a priest (Rev. Beatrice) and to me, a sister teacher, every day. Right from the start we told them that in this program they were going to need to learn to live with others and to communicate truthfully and deeply with their sisters in this training. I placed Reverend Beatrice in charge of the program, and a week later I left with Master Peter for a west coast lecture tour.

During this same period, the concept that maybe Mother Mary wanted me to take celibacy vows kept coming up in my meditations. Lifelong celibacy was something that we were neither expecting nor encouraging in the orders. We recommended that our ministers and even our committed students be conscious and enter into romantic relationships only when and if they received inner guidance to do so. They should allow God to guide those relationships as they developed. When the possibility of my being asked to commit to celibacy was first presented to me in meditation, I found myself having great resistance to it. The idea brought up all kinds of emotions that seemed surprisingly intense. In reality there was no likely candidate for me to marry, and I felt that I needed to be single and free to move about as needed. The voices in me that were resisting celibacy spoke louder and louder, yet, why this became such a battle was an enigma to me.

I entered into myself and asked Mother Mary to please help me see what was going on. I was shown that in a number of my past lives, I was forced to choose between having a family and entering into a deep spiritual life, which was generally only available in monasteries. As a woman in some of those lives, I worked hard and long to try to bring about changes that would allow women to marry, have children, *and* take on full spiritual authority. Now, finally, our Order had provided a place where a woman could, in fact, do all of those. Since it was available, why was I being asked to take vows of celibacy? I felt my soul crying out. It felt so unfair. The opportunity to express fully through marriage, mothering, profession, and spiritual service simultaneously was going to be available to everyone except me. Moses must have felt that way when after 40 years in the desert, he got close enough to the promised land to see it and yet was told all could enter but he.

Once I saw this and realized why it had felt so big, I reached up to Mother Mary and asked, "Mother Mary, what do you want me to do?"

She answered, "I love you so much that I want you to enter into the company of the virgins." She glowed with love for me as she said this. There I was, on the one hand with what I had worked for over many lifetimes, and on the other the invitation of Mother Mary to enter into something unknown to me. I held those two opposites all day, feeling the immense tension between them, and allowed that tension to grow. Carl Jung said that out of such holding of the two opposites, a third option or solution will arise. I waited, feeling split in half. That evening I went into the chapel. In meditation I was shown that I had asked for God to use me in whatever way I could be of the greatest service to God. I had vowed to follow God's will for me above all my own wishes. Now I was being told I could serve best through taking a vow of celibacy. I fell on my knees and I prayed to Mary: "Mother, I am nothing without you. Take me into the life that you want for me."

A vision opened up before me. Mother Mary descended holding a veil that she then placed on my head. It encircled my whole head, covering my face. It was of a translucent material and had stars throughout it that looked alive and glistened as stars in the sky do. Many women were behind her, smiling at me as she said, "Welcome into the Company of Virgins." This was a term I had never heard before she said it. I knew only what I felt there, that I was once again a virgin, a term that has been interpreted as meaning "one unto oneself," and that there was something quite wonderful being offered by entering into this life of celibacy under Mother Mary. I completely let go of my attachment to having the right to partake of the fruits of my labors, which brought women the opportunity to simultaneously be priests, teachers, mothers, and spouses. Mother Mary seemed to have something different in mind for me. She had never misled me before. I was now willing to give my life over to her will for me.

I called Master Peter the next day. I said that Mother Mary told me to ask him whether he would receive my vows. I explained that she had also said that my vows were to be for life, unless she at some point told me otherwise. Master Peter was moved and said he would be glad to receive my vows when he was in Boston in a few days. That weekend, while Master Peter taught a class in our living room, I went upstairs to the chapel. As I meditated, I became painfully clear that God was offering me a great gift and that I had been blind and dense in refusing to see what a gift it was. I felt a deep remorse and sadness that I had not immediately trusted God entirely but instead had held onto my own ideas and dreams. I went downstairs and asked Master Peter to take my confession. I knelt down and poured out my grief at having been so slow to accept Mother Mary and the Creator's Love for me through the taking of this vow. Master Peter absolved me and blessed me.

We went up to the chapel. The students and the ministers, Rev. Beatrice and Deacon Marcella, were all there in prayer and meditation. Master Peter waited for my directions on how we were to proceed. I played a recording of a beautiful Latin musical piece called *Totus tuus sum Maria,* which in English is "I am entirely yours, Mary." The power in the room intensified. We prayed 10 "Hail Mary" prayers. I then knelt, and Master Peter accepted my vow, the words of which I had received from Mother Mary. The tears poured down my face as I spoke the words, not because I did not want to take this vow, but because of my grief at having resisted. I was also letting go of all past attachments. The presence of Mother Mary in the room was overwhelming. As people left the chapel to go home, they were speechless. When we asked them what they experienced, they all spoke of witnessing me taking those vows as the most powerful spiritual presence and experience they had ever had. They were awed and silenced in the beauty, power, and love that Mother Mary had poured down on me that night. I was happy that they were able to receive a bit of it, too. I could not speak of any of it for more than a day; I was still in that altered state of being in the presence of Mother Mary and being brought into her court. I knew without a doubt that I had been truly blessed beyond all measure.

The Order Grows and Guidance is Received to Move to Seattle

By New Year's, 2000, it was clear that my house in Needham was too small to shelter the growing number of people coming to classes and Sunday services. We found a huge Victorian house just minutes away in Newton and moved in on February 7th. We now had an average of 12 people coming on Sundays, who brought with them half a dozen children. We arranged childcare during the services and invited all the children to receive communion. We now had room for more novices, too. Our living-room-turned-chapel could hold about 40 people, so we felt like we should have enough space for a while. The Milwaukee group was growing, too. The weekends on which we had workshops were getting more and more attendance. We felt we were right on the edge of a big growth spurt. We now offered two five-day retreats a year in which all the students and ministers got together from both centers. The atmosphere was one of excitement and of people feeling immensely blessed to have come across these teachings and this order.

Master Peter and I take a week to go away and meditate and write our lectures before each retreat. These times have proven to be powerful in that new directives are given to us for the Order and entirely new emphases can be developed. During such a week in December 2000, to our great surprise, we received guidance that in August I was to move to Seattle, and that in October Master Peter was to move to the San Francisco Bay Area. We also were told to invite certain deacons to move with us to those two areas and help start new centers there. When we returned to Boston and Milwaukee and told the students and the ministers the news of our leaving, they were stunned. Some expressed shock and grief, some fear of things falling apart without us, and some excitement that the Order was to grow from having two centers to having four after only two years in existence. It was a major new development. These two centers were now strong enough to be on their own without us. We assured them that we would be back once each month and would be continuing to stay in very close touch over the phone.

Reverend Beatrice was to be in charge of the Boston Center and Reverend Catherine, the Milwaukee Center. We also got guidance that there were no longer to be two orders, but just the Order of Christ/Sophia. We were told that all the purposes and aims of the Holy Order of Sophia had been adopted by the Order of Christ/Sophia: Women were being supported and empowered to take on spiritual authority, and their blockages from doing so were explored and addressed. In addition, the Order of Christ/Sophia was also serving and training men and supporting the gender specific issues for them, too. As evidence of the Order of Christ/Sophia's support of women in spiritual authority, the first two priests, who would be in the charge of the centers when Master Peter and I left, were both women.

The deacons who were invited to move with us to the west coast all got inner guidance to come, and were quite excited about this new development. My students from the early years, Marcella, her husband Tim, and their three young children prepared to move with me to Seattle. Four single deacons, two from Boston and two from Milwaukee, prepared to move with Master Peter to the Bay Area. We found and bought houses in both places and doubled up on our training of those who would be staying to prepare them to take on those responsibilities.

Preparation for and Ordination as a Master Teacher

In March 2001, Master Peter told me that he had received Guidance that he was to ordain me a master teacher on the last day of June, during the summer retreat. He explained to me that this was an entirely new level I would be entering into, and that I was not obligated to take it on. I should consider it seriously. I had at that time been a sister teacher for two years, and I had felt the great teachers from the invisible realms and Jesus and Mary working on me and stretching me toward higher levels of functioning. I asked guidance and was told that I was to accept the offer to be ordained a master teacher. Master Peter began teaching me the lessons that were created for preparing people for mastery. As he began each class, I felt myself taken right up into another world. The intensity was beyond words. Yet I knew I was being led by those who had never misguided me, and I knew I was safe.

Master Peter told me to keep that last month before my ordination open because I would be spending most of it in meditation. The meditations were specific and were given to me to do for the 30 days preceding ordination. They were accompanied by lessons, again written just for that purpose. Three one-hour meditations a day, extensive journaling of my experiences in meditation, and the usual communion and evening prayers did not leave much time for anything else. Those 30 days took me through everything left in my being that I needed to examine, understand, and transform. It was so intense I could not actually speak with anyone except Master Peter during that month. The hosts and angels were so close, and Jesus and Mary were overseeing and guiding my every meditation and prayer.

Three days before ordination, I went into seclusion in a Franciscan Monastery near the retreat center where the ordination would take place. During those three days of fasting, meditation, and prayer, every last part of my heart, mind, and soul were examined by the Archangels, by the Brothers and Sisters in White, and by Jesus and Mary, before I was to be lifted up to working with them as a master teacher. They filled me with their instruction, their support and their love. By the morning of the ordination, I felt immensely humbled and amazed by the constancy and power of their love, and the beauty of how they had led me to this point and had never let me down.

During the ordination, I was asked a series of questions that attested to my having moved into the heaven worlds and demonstrated that I acquired answers to what is there based on my own experience. All true master teachers are so tested and queried so that they must prove their direct relationship to the hosts and to the angels and show that they have found the truth of all ages for themselves. The ordaining master will have already ascertained this before the ordination, but in the ordination it is publicly attested to. Master Peter was clearly full of joy to be bringing me into this level of service. He was the only one there who knew for himself what this was about, so it felt somewhat like he and I were alone with the heavenly host. All those beings from the heaven world who had been teaching me and guiding me through the preparation period were there in support and in celebration. I had no fear or worry because I knew that I was, of my own self, nothing, and all that I had was because they gave it to me. After the ordination was finished, I stood while one after the other the ministers and students came up to hug me. Many were teary and said they were overwhelmed with the intensity of the presence of other beings in the room. Others spoke of their immense sense of awe at the level of being and service that I was taking on, and their gratitude at having been able to witness this moment. The circle of love that surrounded me felt strong and complete, both in heaven and on Earth. I was overwhelmed with gratitude and joy that I was allowed to serve in this way. The 30 days that preceded this event and the ordination itself were a blessing that changed me for the rest of my life.

I gave the sermon the next day. I spoke on love. Tears poured down my cheeks as I tried to tell everyone there how much they were loved. I said, "If you only knew how loved you are, you would never be afraid again." I told them that God's love is so immense that absolutely everything at all times comes under it. Jesus and Mary's love is added to that. In addition, there is the love of all the teachers and hosts on the other side, in the heaven world. I tried with all my heart to impart this great truth that had been demonstrated to me. Most of the congregation wept with me. Even though they were not yet in a place to know this reality for themselves, as I now did, they gratefully accepted my testimony, longing for the day they would personally experience the great love that is God.

The Order Grows to Include Centers in Eight States

In August of that year I moved to Seattle, and Master Peter moved to Oakland in October. The deacons who moved with us also began to settle in. We started offering classes, and once again we had chapels in our homes. Our group felt small and intimate, like the beginnings of things in Boston. The Milwaukee and Boston centers continued to grow after our departures from them and, in fact, seemed to thrive due to the priests there taking on more authority. The Boston Christ/Sophia Center ran out of room in their chapel, and in the spring of 2002 rented a much larger space for services, classes, and workshops. A deacon living in New Haven, Connecticut, began to teach and serve there, and later was ordained a priest and was named Reverend David. In the early spring of 2003, Reverends William and Margaret, a priest couple from Milwaukee, moved to Denver to start a center. Three weeks later Reverend Beatrice and a deacon who in 2003 became Reverend Ruth moved to Dallas to start a center. And in the fall of that same year, a minister couple, Reverend Cynthia and Deacon Phillip from Boston, bought a house in Atlanta and moved there to start a center. We all knew this was just the beginning. We now had centers in eight states and the order was only four years old.

Sermon On Mastery Ordination

The following is the sermon I gave the morning after my ordination as a master teacher.

Sermon July 1, 2001
Rt. Rev. Clare Watts
West Bend, WI

Reading from the Gospel of John, Chapter 17, verses 1-25:

Having spoken these words, Jesus looked up to heaven and said, "Father-Mother, the hour has come; glorify your Son so that the Son may glorify you, since you have given that Son authority over all people, to give eternal life to all whom you have given your Son. And this is eternal life, that they may know you, the only true God, and Jesus Christ whom you have sent. I glorified you on earth by finishing the work that you gave me to do. So now, Father/Mother, glorify Me in your own presence with the glory that I had in your presence before the world existed.

"I have made your name known to those whom you gave me from the world. They were yours, and you gave them to me, and they have kept your word. Now they know that everything that you have given me is from you; for the words that you gave to me I have given to them, and they have received the words that you gave to me and they know the truth that I came from you; they have believed that you sent Me. I am asking on their behalf; I am not asking on the behalf of the world but on the behalf of those whom you gave me, because they are Yours. All Mine are Yours, and Yours are Mine; and I have been glorified in them. And now I am no longer in the world, but they are in the world, and I am coming to you. Holy Father/Mother, protect them in your name that you have given me, so that they may be one, as we are one. While I was with them, I protected them in your name. I guarded them, and not one of them was lost except the one destined to be lost, so that the scriptures might be fulfilled. But now I am coming to you, and I speak these things in the world so that they may have My joy made complete in them. I have given them Your word, and the world has hated them because they do not belong to the world, just as I do not belong to the world. I'm not asking You to take them out of the world, but I ask you to protect them from the evil one. They do not belong to the world, just as I do not belong to the world. Sanctify them, Father/Mother, in the truth; Your word is truth. As you have sent Me into the world, so I have sent them into the world. And for their sakes I sanctify myself, so that they also might be sanctified in truth.

"I ask not only on behalf of these, but also on behalf of those who will believe in me through their word, that they may all be one. As you Father/

Mother are in Me and I am in You, may they also be in Us, so that the world will believe that you have sent Me. The glory that you have given Me I have given them, so that they may be one, as We are One, I in them and You in Me, that they may become completely one, so that the world may know that you have sent me and have loved them even as you have loved Me. Father/Mother, I desire that those also whom you have given Me, may be with Me where I am, to see My Glory, which you have given Me because You loved Me before the foundation of the world.

"Righteous Father/Mother, the world doesn't know you, but I know you; and these know that You have sent Me. I made Your name known to them, and I will make it known, so that the love with which You have loved Me may be in them, and I in them."

My sermon:

"I didn't sleep much last night because I had mixed emotions. On the one hand, I wanted so very much to bring this message to you this morning, and on the other hand, I felt so concerned and afraid that I wouldn't be able to. What was weighing on me was that Jesus and Mary have spent their existences trying to bring this same message to you, and to the world, and very few people have been able to hear Them. So why should I believe that anybody could hear me? But I was getting guidance that I still need to try, and I need to spend my lifetimes trying.

So, in order to try to get this to you, I want to tell you about my experience of my ordination yesterday. Most of you know that we don't usually speak about our ordinations or initiations. But I want to try, through speaking of it, to have some bit of a chance to break through to you what it is I am trying to tell you. I think you all know that I spent the 27 days before the ordination in a lot of meditation each day. And then I spent three days in seclusion. During this time there was one solid, constant theme. It was so clear and so strong, that it then carried into the ordination and it became the theme of the ordination.

The theme is this: You cannot imagine how much you are loved. If you only got it, you would never worry again. You would never be afraid again. If you just knew. If you just opened to receive it. You don't need to be anything, anything. I was not ordained because I am something. I was ordained because I am nothing. You are all already nothing, if you could just get comfortable with that. You are already there. Stop fighting it. Know that in your nothingness you are loved beyond all measure. The angels filled this place and kneeled by me, with me, at my ordination because of the glory of the plan that God takes us, who are nothing, and raises us up into heaven.

How, how will God get this through to you? How will God break your hearts open? How will God still your minds of their constant arguing? When will you let God love you? When will you stop trying to prove your case against yourself to God? It is so profound, the miracle that we are so loved, and we need to be nothing but that nothingness that we already are. We are so taken care of; it seems unbelievable.

Tons of angels stand to wait on us hand and foot, and yet we freak out about every little thing, things we usually have no control over anyhow. And we get in the way of God's love for us hundreds of times every day. And the angels weep for the wasted love. They don't know what else to do for you. They have offered you everything. When Master Peter and I went back to the log house last night I said, "Peter, how are we going to tell them? How will we get it across how much they are loved?"

There is nothing in your way to coming into the presence of God but your own arguing against it. I assure you I have no special gifts of any kind. And don't even start arguing against that in your own heads! Because if you are arguing my statement that I have no special gifts, you are just making your argument for your separation from God. God doesn't need us to be anything or to do anything but surrender to God's love. To throw ourselves into the arms of love and let God take care of us. Let God show us what's going to fill our lives with joy. Let God show us the way. I feel it's almost arrogant of me to try to get this across. The Master wept many times over the inability to crack through human hearts with that message of love. He still weeps over it. He does not weep over your petty little problems. He doesn't care about your petty little problems. Why do you care? It's all taken care of for you.

As I prepared for the ordination, the Great Beings from the other side came to me and asked me if there was anything else I needed. "Are you okay? Will you be okay?" they asked. They didn't come and say: "You little piece of dirt! What do you think you are doing here?" They did not beat me into the ground. Isn't that what we think They are going to do? They said: "What else can we do for you? How else can we love you and support you?"

They are there saying the same to you, all the time. "Let us help you. Give us your burdens. Turn it over." "Let not your hearts be troubled," said our Master. In the passage I read He said, speaking to God: "For You have loved them as You have loved Me from the beginning." How did Jesus become so great? Because He allowed God to love Him that much. The only thing I have done, maybe more than you have done, is allowed God to love me, not because I thought I deserved it. I knew I didn't, but I knew that whether I deserved it or not was beside the point. Can you dismantle the mechanisms in your minds and your hearts that keep God out? Can you just turn them over? Can you do it today?

I'm feeling my Baptist roots coming up in me. I want to say: "Who will come up here and kneel down and accept Jesus as your Savior?" There is something to that, you know? And I actually want to ask you to do that in this communion. Not later; it doesn't have to take you a long time. That's a con-coction of your thinking again. Can you, when you kneel here to receive communion, actually go: "Enough! I don't need to do this anymore. I give my life over completely, without reservation." Can you then open that space and let

God's love completely fill you? Take it into your life as the guiding force in your life, not the fear altar at which you worship, or your worry or control altars at which you worship. Burn those altars and worship at the altar of the Love of God. I challenge you to that this day, and I know that sounds a little Baptist here. Do it now. What the hell (literally) are you waiting for? You don't need to indulge it anymore. It has cost you enough pain already, enough separation from God. Enough.

So, when you get on your knees, give it over, open in that communion to take it in completely. Make a commitment from as deep down as you can go and with your total being to no longer refuse God's love; to become content with being nothing, and to be sustained only by God's love. And that you will allow that Love to be enough for you for all eternity.

May the love of our Mother Mary descend upon you. May She give you the courage, the faith, the hope to turn it all over, to Her, to Master Jesus, and to our Creator. To enter into a full love relationship with your Creator, Who has loved you from the beginning of all time. In the names of Jesus and Mary, let this be done. In the name of the Creator, the Mediators, and the Holy Spirit, Amen."

Living in God

My experience of life in God is that God now guides each day and each of my actions. Through coming to know God within my being and allowing Him/Her to fill me completely from within, I actually feel constantly that I am living in God. It is a life where pleasant events and less pleasant events still happen. Some moments feel frustrating when something isn't working, and some feel sad, as when a student gives up. But the backdrop and underlying feeling—at all times—is deep peace and joy.

When you live in God it means you have given over your will and desires into the service of God. You have developed a complete trust in God through numerous experiences. You have come to know the love of God as the source of everything you need. You now know that God's love is immeasurably abundant, so you never fear any lack. You have come to feel how much God loves all the human beings on earth, and as God is living in and through you, you feel that same love for them. As God seeks to give us everything to bring us into peace and joy with Him/Her, so you, once you have entered into life in God, seek to do the same for your fellow humans.

You have read my stories. You have seen that I was not different from other people, except from those who do not long for and seek out God and let God love them. That is the only distinguishing factor between me and those who have not risen to the heights of spiritual experience and grace. Jesus promised us, "Ask and you shall receive. Seek and you shall find. Knock and it will be opened to you." That is what I did. Again, as Jesus promised, "Blessed are the poor in spirit, for theirs is the dominion of God." I wanted nothing more, so I became poor in spirit, not holding onto things. I knew I needed help to find my way to union with God, and I was given the dominion of God. I allowed the teachers on Earth and my teachers in heaven, Jesus and Mary, to grind me down and wash me clean until I was pure in heart, and as Jesus said, "Blessed are the pure in heart, for they shall see God." I do see God. Jesus and Mary did not intend for their great blessings to be for the elite alone. They loved the simple people, the shepherds, the farmers, and the housewives. Jesus and Mary found no place in the hearts of most of the learned and the accomplished. It is still the same now. Insomuch as you can be simple and humble, and you can want nothing more than to know and serve God, you can rise to the heights of spiritual life. We see it all the time in the Order: The simple and dedicated move swiftly and unencumbered along their way toward God. There is a Chinese saying: "The journey of a thousand miles begins with a single step." You do have to take that step, or your journey will never begin. You don't have to understand it all in advance. You don't have to know what you will do later on down the Path. You could not possibly know that now, because when you get there, you will be different, and you will understand everything differently.

My prayers and blessings are upon every reader of this book. May you find your way to a teacher. May you have the humility to allow that teacher to love you and teach you, and when the time is right, may you find your way into the very heart of God, and be in peace.

BIBLIOGRAPHY

Buber, Martin. "Tales of the Hasidim." New York: Schocken Books.

Lao Tsu. "Tao Te Ching." Translation by Gia-Fu Feng and Jane English. Vintage Books.

"New Testament. Inclusive Version." Oxford Press.

Schimmel, Annemarie. "The Mystical Dimensions of Islam." Chapel Hill.

Rumi, Jalalu'ddin. "The Mathnawi." Luzac & Co, London.

Murray, W.H. "The Scottish Himalayan Expedition." J.M. Dent & Sons, Ltd.

0-595-28337-3

Printed in the United States
112038LV00003B/226-282/A

9 780595 283378